D1635179

SHADOW BEHIND THE SUN

Remzije Sherifi
With Robert Davidson

FOREWORD BY GEORGE SZIRTES

Sandstone Press
Highland, Scotland

SHADOW BEHIND THE SUN

First published 2007 in Great Britain by Sandstone Press Ltd
PO Box 5725, 1 High Street, Dingwall, Ross-shire, IV15 9WJ.

Copyright © Remzije Sherifi with Robert Davidson 2007
Foreword Copyright © George Szirtes 2007

ISBN: 978-1-905207-13-8

The moral right of Remzije Sherifi with Robert Davidson to be
identified as the author of this work has been asserted in
accordance with the Copyright, Design and Patents Act, 1988.

Cover image and map by Artan Sherifi.

Designed and typeset in ITC Giovanni by River Design, Edinburgh.

Scottish **Arts** Council

The publisher acknowledges subsidy from the Scottish Arts
Council towards the publication of this volume.

Printed and bound in the European Union.

ABERDEENSHIRE LIBRARY AND INFORMATION SERVICES	
2576498	
HJ	542923
L949.71	£9.95
AD	ALW

CONTENTS

ACKNOWLEDGEMENTS

Remzije Sherifi would like to thank everyone who has helped her and her family. Many of them are mentioned in *Shadow Behind The Sun*. Thanks also to all those who work with dispossessed and displaced people everywhere, and the asylum seekers who have enriched her life.

She acknowledges with gratitude the many people who have contributed to the creation of this book: Artan (of course), Jo Haythornethwaite who introduced her to Sandstone Press, Moira Forsyth who commented on the developing text, Kirstie Gordon who contributed the use of her flat, Iain and Bridget Gordon, and with a very special acknowledgment to the doctors and staff of Stobhill Hospital.

DEDICATION

For all of those who lost their lives through the generations in Kosova, all those who were jailed, persecuted and disappeared during the war, all those who have been separated from their families, and for all those obliged to leave their home country and begin new lives elsewhere. For my husband, sons and wider family.

In special memory of my sister, Sherife.

AUTHOR'S NOTE AND PRONUNCIATION GUIDE

For historical reasons most maps of Kosova give place names in Serbo-Croat. Most of the population though, have an Albanian heritage and speak in the Kosovar version of Albanian. In this book I have chosen to use Albanian names. To aid understanding, there follows a list of Albanian place and people's names with a pronunciation guide. RS

PLACES

Albanian	Phonetic
Banja e Siarinës	Ban-ya e See-ar-ee-nus
Blacë	Blatch
Cerrcë	Tzir-zi
Dardana	Dar-dana
Deçan	De-tchan
Ferizaj	Fer-ee-zai
Gjakova	Jack-oh-va
Gjilan	Jee-lan
Graçanicë	Grah-chah-neeti
Furshë Kosova	Foorsh Kosova
Kaçanik	Ka-tcha-nik
Keqekollë	Ketch-e-kole
Koliqi	Koh-lee-chi
Lepenc	Le-pentz
Likoshan	Lick-oh-shan
Llasticë	Lash-teetzi
Nish	Neesh
Peja	Pay-ah
Prapashticë	Prap-ash-tee-tchi

Prekaz i Ultë	Preh-kahz i Oolt
Priluzhie	Pree-loo-zhia
Prishtinë	Prish-tee-na
Prizeren	Pree-ze-ren
Raçak	Rah-tchak
Rahovec	Rah-ho-vetz
Skopje	Skop-yeh
Split	Split
Stankovec	Stank-oh-vetz
Svircë	Svee-irtz
Tivar	Tee-var
Trepça	Trep-tchi
Ulqin	Ool-chin
Vitia	Vee-tee-a
Vukovar	Voo-ko-var

PEOPLE

Afërdita	Ah-fer-deeta
Afiz	Ah-feez
Agani	Ah-gah-ni
Ahmet	Ah-met
Arkan	Ar-kan
Bojaxhiu	Boy-ah-jee-oo
Çaushi	Chah-oo-shay
Doda	Doad-ah
Emin	Ay-meen
Fehime	Feh-hee-mi
Fehmi	Feh-me
Gërvalla	Gr-vala
Gjyle	Jew-li

Gongje	Goan-ji
Hajdin	Hai-din
Hamide	Hah-me-di
Hoxhenica	Hodg-en-itsa
Ibrahim	Ee-bra-heem
Idriz	Id-riz
Ilhan	Il-han
Ismet	Is-met
Jashari	Yah-shah-ri
Kaçak	Ka-tchak
Kaçushe	Kah-choo-shi
Karadzic	Ka-rad-jeek
Kolgeci	Call-gay-tzi
Maritca	Ma-ree-tza
Mihailovic	Mee-hy-lo-veetch
Milosevic	My-law-shi-veetch
Mladic	Mla-deetch
Muharrem	Moo-ha-rem
Ramadani	Rah-ma-dani
Remzi	Rehm-zi
Remzije	Rem-zee-yi
Rugova	Roo-go-va
Salihe	Sal-ee-ha
Sejdi	Say-di
Shemsi	Shem-si
Sherife	Sher-ee-fi
Sherifi	Sher-ee-fee
Sheshel	Sheh-shel
Shkëlzen	Shkul-zen
Teuta	Tay-oo-ta
Tunç	Toonsh
Tush	Toosh

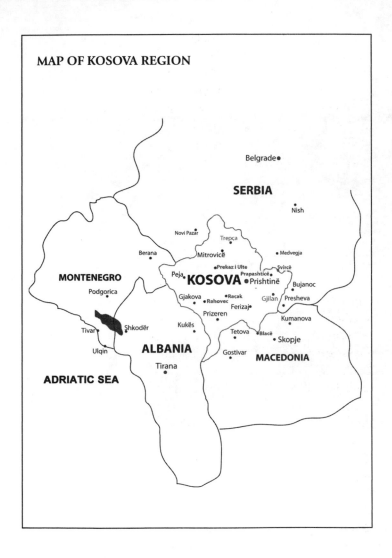

MAP OF KOSOVA REGION

Belgrade

SERBIA

Nish

Novi Pazar

Trepca

Berana

Mitrovicë

Medvegja

Prekaz i Ulte

Svircë

Peja

KOSOVA

Prapashticë

MONTENEGRO

Prishtinë

Bujanoc

Podgorica

Gjakova

Racak

Gjilan

Presheva

Rahovec

Ferizaj

Prizeren

Kumanova

Tivar

Shkodër

Kukës

Tetova

Blacë

Skopje

Ulqin

ALBANIA

Gostivar

MACEDONIA

Tirana

ADRIATIC SEA

FOREWORD

George Szirtes

Any attempt to sort out the political history of Kosova, as of the entire Balkan region, is bound to result in fierce controversy and is certainly not within my own competence. In current parlance, I have no intention of *going there*. I state this upfront since the author of a Foreword is, by implication, committed to the text that follows.

But there are commitments and commitments. Human beings are not distinct from history on either a personal or a social level. They are born into circumstances they have not created – into races, religions, regions, nations, tribes, associations and families – and they carry their histories with them not only on their political backs but in their very genes. Or so it seems, all too painfully and all too frequently. Our commitments to the catalogue of groupings are partly voluntary, partly assumed by others. You are partly what you think you are, but just as often – maybe more often – you are treated on the basis of what others assume you to be. Pogroms, massacres, genocides, holocausts are the result. The fiercest battles are fuelled by the fiercest controversies. As the writer of this terrifying and gripping memoir, Remzije Sherifi, says: 'Time and again I would read of such horrors as I knew were being repeated every day, *and by the descendants of the same people*' (my italics). I will not go where those italics lead me nor is it my business to go there. I can neither affirm nor deny that perspective. I can do no more than listen and stand back.

But a commitment to individual human beings and to humanity at large is a different and larger matter. Human beings suffer as individuals. They suffer personally and they suffer an element of the sufferings of others through an ennobling empathy. It is, of course, the suffering of those to whom we can put a name or face that most affects us: family, friends, people familiar in public life. And I cannot quite help thinking that there is a vaguely definable reception range for empathy, a point beyond which empathy moves into what may become self-right-eous sentimentality, an equation in which hatred of the perceived offender becomes equal to or greater than love for the perceived offended. The test will always be in action, usually direct action. The test will be in time, money and energy committed: in food, shelter, protection, and championing through a quiet calling-by-name.

But I am discussing these commitments from the safety of a chair and a desk, in a warm room, looking out at a bright winter sky that is unlikely to carry the echo of approaching gunfire or the fear of imminent murder and rape. It is very different for those who live, or have recently lived, under less secure skies, as the writer of *Shadow Behind the Sun* has done.

In 1991 I was one of two British writers invited to attend the literary festival at Struga, Macedonia, just as the troubles of the former Yugoslavia were beginning. The American writers who should have attended were advised not to. We flew into Belgrade on the day that President Gorbachev was being set free from house arrest at his dacha. The next morning we flew to Ohrid in a small plane that leapfrogged the mountains and banked quite sharply over Lake Ohrid before returning to land at the rough and ready airport. The landscape around Struga and Ohrid is spectacular, with some magnificent Orthodox churches and monasteries. Our English-speaking guide said he was expecting trouble soon all over the country, even, he said, in Macedonia.

The terrors were to come shortly after, terrors on top of historical terrors I had only read about. Like other people in the West I watched the siege of Sarajevo and heard the reports of murders, burnings alive, massacres, tortures and concentration camps. Then came the NATO forces and the air-raids on Belgrade, and little by little the disintegration of the Milosevic regime with its schemes of Greater Serbia.

The idea of Greater Serbia spelled trouble in the region, much as the idea Greater Hungary would do, for there was, and remains, a movement for Greater Hungary too. The proponents of that movement point to gross historical injustices, as irredentist movements have always done, and for perfectly comprehensible reasons. In the case of Hungary it was the reduction of the country by two-thirds of its geographical area together with the loss of half its population by the Treaty of Trianon after 1919. Whole families were split up. Areas associated with legend and culture were suddenly abroad, in hostile territory. In 1995 in Budapest as a journalist I attended an open-air political meeting where people could buy postcard maps of the whole region. You pulled a tab at the side of the postcard and the area of pre-1919 Greater Hungary popped up.

Enormous passions and loyalties are prompted by such memories and, as Sherifi says more than once, and indeed exemplifies in her own writing, memories in the Balkans are particularly long and engaged. Who would believe such atavistic monstrosities could be visited neighbour on neighbour in the last years of the century in Europe? They were though. They might be again.

Sherifi's book offers a close eye-witness account to something of what happened in Kosova in the mid-1990s. Beyond that it is a family story and a community story, one that tells of serious illness as well as ethnic aggression and violence. It is a story of survival. But then again it is something more than that too. It is a tale of refugees and asylum seekers, every second chapter in the book being a report on life in refugee communities in Glasgow. It tells of organisation and support and in doing so it argues for humanitarian values: for welcome, for kindness, for efficiency and sensitivity. As the book goes on, it records events in places like the Drop-In Centre and the Oasis Women's Group, and talks of the coming together of people of very different backgrounds, as when a Christian Gospel group is brought in to entertain an audience 'mostly made up of Turkish Kurds, Muslims' that ends up in a conga danced round the Community Hall.

The commitment to those hurt, traumatised, exiled and derelict is both universal and personal, just as the account that follows this is. A face emerges out of the turbulent waters of history and speaks to us of where it has been. Dangerous waters leave few survivors. We must look after those that find themselves aboard our own apparently so-solid ship. There is no unsinkable ship, there are only boats and rafts in history. Looking after them is looking after ourselves. Is, indeed, being ourselves. We need people such as Remzije Sherifi to speak out of the waters and help us be ourselves.

SHADOW BEHIND THE SUN

ABOVE THE DROP-IN CAFÉ

Four square and solid in its permanence, this building gives the impression that certain things can be relied on and will not change.

The people I work with are glad of this. Like me they are among those of the world who have known all too much change. My office is very small, located at the top of a narrow, winding, wooden stair. The room contains only the sort of furniture you would expect, filing cabinets, shelving. Like the building my desk was designed by Charles Rennie Mackintosh and, although it is covered by so many files and notes I can hardly see its surface, I love it. Along with pictures of my husband and sons the shelves hold some of the cups and plates I decorate with flower and other patterns, some of the cards I make, a few potted plants. Photographs of amateur fashion shows and dance groups are pinned to the wall. Piles of paper are everywhere because there is no end to form filling.

The only window looks down on the yard and across its short width to the back of a tenement block. Paved with flagstones and walled off from the street, the yard is never used. It is afternoon and sunlight streams across the tenement roof to brighten the geranium and spider plant on my window ledge.

On the floor below people take refuge behind the solid wooden door of the Drop-In Café. They are asylum seekers and refugees, as I once was, but they feel safe here. The city thinks of itself as enlightened and in many ways it is, but it is also one of the most deprived in Britain and this is one of its poorest areas. There are people among our host community who do not tolerate difference easily and the asylum seekers and refugees are certainly different: vulnerable and weak, often frightened.

Inevitably their numbers will increase.

It is the summer of 2006 and tanks are rolling again in the Middle East. Rockets fly across borders and bombing campaigns are pursued mercilessly. Elsewhere in the world armies are locked in combat, civilians are murdered in industrial numbers, territories are cleared. Whole populations are on the move. When those who are seeking asylum arrive it is generally in London and from there they are dispersed 'without choice' to various cities that, for their own reasons, have decided they should accept some proportion of the whole. After that their cases are considered by the Home Office and, if accepted, they become refugees. With that status they enter a new set of rights and obligations. With the world as it is the asylum seekers are a never ending stream.

I work steadily here in Glasgow with individuals and their families. Various officials stop by from time to time to check on things, and I think they enjoy their visits. We keep things going and have enough success to carry us through some heartbreaking partings and tragic ends of which the public is mostly unaware.

People find it difficult to look at what they don't want to see. It is easier by far to ignore than to examine present needs and what might be the portents of a violent future. Of course they are also wary of the unknown, of different physical types and dress. Natural barriers exist, such as language; other barriers are erected. It is all too easy to stigmatise, even as the asylum seekers struggle to adapt and make the beginnings of a new life in almost impossible circumstances.

Understanding is everything. To examine one life in detail, and to extend out through others, could be sufficient, at least for some, a few. I sit behind my desk and cast my mind back to Kosova.

LOOKING TO THE FUTURE

We built a house in Gjilan, on the hills behind the town; but those were difficult and changing times.

With my husband's arms around me and our baby son in mine I had no fear of the future. It was a warm summer's day and we looked down onto the town's roofs that together resembled a great red blanket thrown across the surrounding green of fields and tree-covered hills. The hill closest, we knew, held an underground base used by the Yugoslav army, at that time made up of soldiers from every ethnic group in Yugoslavia. Behind the base sat the village of Malisheva, with a uniformly Albanian population, and behind that again lay Shillova, which was mostly Serbian.

Our part of Kosova had a significant minority of Serb citizens but we had coexisted more or less happily all through my lifetime. Each community had its own language and customs and, although there was little intermarriage, we were educated together, worked and played together. Fourteen years later another village close to us, Llasticë, would be attacked the night before we were. Malisheva would be attacked at the same time.

We had just bought the land we were standing on and were about to build our new home here. There were a hundred building plots for sale and one had already been taken by my sister Sherife and her husband Ferat. Their sons, Albert and Adonis, would be companions for our three. Below us and very close was the large house that my uncles lived in with my cousins Shemsi and Afërdita. Already they were planning to extend into the adjacent ground. All around were green spaces and fresh air for the boys, safe places for them to play and that would benefit my mother-in-law, Fehime, who suffered from asthma. And, at last, I would have the garden I longed for.

From here we could see my old school; the upholstery factory from which my husband travelled as International Sales Manager; the sports centre where he used to coach handball; the radio station where I worked, which was the highest building in Gjilan. In the centre of town were our own flat and, not far away, my parents' home, and the town square with the theatre and community centre. Here were our lives. We had been married for six years, and could not have been happier. This was our place and it held all the warmth and goodness of home. We had no foreboding of the terrible events ahead. I put the toddler down to join his two brothers.

We felt secure in our love for each other and in our family. The prospect of our future in this new place thrilled me but we were in no hurry to complete our house, content to build slowly towards our future. All around us builders were at work. Ditches were being dug and concrete foundations going in. Paths and water mains and electricity cables were being laid.

At home I sketched my ideas for our new home in the blank back pages of a cook book. Following the tradition of the region the roof would be red and the walls white. There would be five levels, three looking out to Gjilan and the view we had been admiring that day. I saw no need to include a basement. Most importantly, the boys could have their own apartments as they grew. They might even begin their married lives here and that would surely be the answer to a new grandmother's prayer. If they moved away there would be plenty of room for them to return on long visits. This is how far I looked ahead and this is how hope works in the human heart.

My husband examined my sketches and nodded. Yes, he could go along with my thinking. 'We will have more space than we ever dreamed of, and our boys will have room to grow,' he said, smiling. 'Yes, we can be happy in a house like this.' Next day he took my sketches to an architect and instructed that the house plans be drawn accordingly.

The following spring construction began and every weekend I visited to see how it was progressing. New neighbours, some of whom had already built their houses, came along to introduce themselves, some young, some older; a new community was forming. In our enthusiasm and hope we were not to know that thirteen long years would pass before we entered the house to live, or that our stay would be so very brief.

My parents were Albanians, like the great majority of the region's population. They began their married life in the Kosovan Highlands around Svircë and moved to Prishtinë after the Second World War. There Sherife was born with brother Ismet soon following. My sister Hevzija arrived next, but she died in the year I was born. I have no memories of her but I know that my parents gave thanks for my safe arrival with broken hearts. After me came Ahmet and then in 1960, when I was five years old, we moved as a family to Gjilan where my youngest brother Agim was born.

I remember my schooldays happily for their many friendships. One I made then, Teuta, is still my best friend although we are separated by thousands of miles. I enjoyed school and excelled academically as did my sister and my brothers. My family, like most people in Gjilan, spoke Albanian. I was taught in Albanian, unlike my older brother and sister who were taught in the official language of the State, Serbo-Croat. About the time I entered school greater language rights were being established so for me Serbo-Croat was a separate subject.

6

In those days Gjilan held a mixture of nationalities. The largest group, as in all Kosova, was ours – Albanians. But there was also a significant minority of Serbians. Added to these were a number of Turkish families and other ethnic groups. Intermarriage between the groups was rare but did happen. Despite the different languages spoken in the home we all went to the same school and socialised together.

When I was sixteen I was chosen as the representative of my school to go to Belgrade for the celebrations of President Tito's birthday. Young people from all the different nationalities that made up Yugoslavia came together in a spectacular parade with music and colour that made a strong impression on me as an expression of youthful unity.

As one of the best students in my school I was selected as a member of the Communist Party. One day one of the teachers told me that I had to go to a meeting. This is how new party members were recruited; there was no application form. You were just invited to get your red member's card. I rarely attended the meetings.

Towards the end of my school life came a day that opened the path to my career and my future life. Since the borders were created in 1912 after the Balkans War, the oldest population of the region, the Albanians, had been artificially divided by the borders of four countries, Serbia, Montenegro, Macedonia and Albania. In the settlement of the First World War the first three of these had been incorporated into the new Yugoslavia, then known as the Kingdom of Serbs, Croats and Slovenes. Although we shared a language and our cultural roots with the Albanians to the south we were never allowed to meet them as we did the nationalities of Yugoslavia.

Now a thaw was happening and, for the first time, the

Professional Government Music Ensemble of Albania was allowed to tour in Kosova. When they arrived in Gjilan it was a big event and the audience was excited. The atmosphere was almost that of a family reunion after a long separation. This was the first step to opening the doors to cultural links with Albania and came only three years after the establishment of the Albanian university in Prishtinë. I was asked to do the simultaneous translation of the speeches and songs of the evening into Serbo-Croat. My translation, I later learned, was not for the audience, made up entirely of Kosovar Albanians, but for the government officials who were monitoring the performance and who were Serbian.

I had never experienced anything like it. Not only was I speaking in front of a full theatre but also meeting famous musicians from another country who took me under their wing, including me as part of the show. I felt I had done a good job with the translation and looking in the mirror after the performance, with all the stage make-up the group's artist had put on me, I saw a different side to myself. For the first time I felt I had grown up.

And it was going to continue. In the spring of that same year, 1973, I introduced the region's Culture Festival, the first such festival the government had permitted in many years. I was very proud and excited to be able to present the acts in our own language. One of the judges was also the music producer for a new regional radio station which was being formed in Gjilan and he approached me and told me about auditions to become a radio presenter. That summer we went on a family holiday to the beach at Ulqin in Montenegro where I enjoyed diving, swimming and sunbathing. Then, on our return, I auditioned at the radio station and was offered a job. I was the youngest member of staff and, since I still had a year of school to finish, I worked at the station only part time.

Soon I had to choose what subject to study at university. I felt drawn to the arts and creativity but my father believed that sort of work could always be done as a hobby. He suggested I do something practical so I started my degree in Electrical Engineering at Prishtinë University in the autumn of 1974. Throughout my time there I continued to build up my journalism and editing skills at the radio station. I hosted talk shows and phone-ins, directed radio plays and programmes for children, and played the music of the time, Diana Ross, Elton John, Deep Purple. In those early days the station didn't have proper recording facilities and had to use a room in the fire station while we were waiting for our studios to be built. This meant lots of hilarious evenings stopping and starting our recordings while we waited for traffic to pass or dogs to stop barking. Two years went past and I became increasingly certain that electrical engineering was not for me. In 1976 I left university to work full time at Radio Gjilan. Journalism and editing became my career.

The programmes from Radio Gjilan went out in Albanian, Serbo-Croat, Turkish and Roma, in time slots proportional to the populations. At that time there was good communication between the editorial teams and we had weekly meetings on Monday mornings. One week during the summer the sports journalist was on holiday and I was asked to cover for him. The handball season was about to begin and my Serbian colleague and I went to the sports centre to see how the athletes' preparations for the new season were getting on.

It was a sweltering 30 degrees while we watched the handball team training. I recognised the coach straight away. His sister and his cousin, who was my brother's best friend, had been in my brother's class at school and, as a girl, I had often visited his uncle's house with my mother. He was shouting encouragement to the players on the other side of the hall. My good schoolfriend Muharrem and his brother were training too. Muharrem was the top player in the Gjilan team and one of the best in the Kosovan league. He took a break to chat with me while I was waiting to interview the coach.

In appearance the coach was very tall and smart. I thought that he should know me very well but he didn't seem to recognise me at all. He had an air of dignity and intelligence about him and I felt like a small girl in comparison to his strong presence. We conducted the interview in two languages for our different radio listeners. His mother tongue was Turkish and when I recorded him in Albanian he asked me to check the material for any mistakes. 'It will go out just the way you said it,' I told him. 'I can edit it if need be, but this is just how you said it and I can't intervene but I'll do my best.' His Albanian was perfect.

After the interview I spoke to Muharrem again and learned that the coach was his uncle. He was proud to be his nephew and spoke of him with respect. He was more than simply a coach for the whole team. He taught them not only how to play but also how to behave in public; he was a role model and a leader.

But he hadn't seemed to recognise me. When I went home I said to my brother that this man seemed to be quite full of himself and a bit too businesslike and formal. My brother defended him, saying he was naturally confident and that was his way. 'It's simple, he didn't recognise you. Since you grew up as my young sister he probably didn't really notice you.'

Unknown to me, a few days later the coach asked Muharrem who I was and I soon started receiving messages that he wanted to meet me. Muharrem started to tease me by calling me auntie. He had it all worked out and was sure that we would be together, but I still didn't reply to the messages. I never had secrets from my best friend Teuta so I let her know what was going on. She knew the coach and said he was wonderful and encouraged me to meet him. But I still didn't reply.

A few months later while I was reading the news live on air I was handed a late item for broadcast. The handball team had gone to the mountains in Montenegro for a game and there had been an accident. Muharrem, known by his second name Gashi, had been struck in the diaphragm by the elbow of one of the other players and had died. I couldn't believe it. My voice started shaking and I had to stop. A colleague had to take over to finish the programme.

I went with Teuta to the funeral, along with more than a thousand people from all over Kosova. Like a shadow behind me I saw the coach looking broken hearted. Muharrem had wanted to arrange a meeting between us and it felt as if I had done something wrong by not going along with his wishes. On that day at the funeral I made the decision that I would meet with him.

After our third meeting he asked me to marry him. This was very early in our relationship but I was already thinking about his qualities. He was very gentle, kind, patient and intelligent. I said to him, 'You are going to be a good father for my children,' and in that way agreed. We got engaged in February 1979, six months after Muharrem's death.

During our engagement we visited each other's homes and sometimes he would join my family on outings to the countryside. My father wasn't sure about the match to begin with but after spending time fishing together they became good friends. I was getting to know him more and gradually becoming more confident and happy in my decision. Preparations began for our wedding.

Sherife was a great organiser and took charge of every detail of the arrangements, from the invitations to preparing the food. Together with my mother and my sister-in-law, Zana, she worked to make my day special. All through her life my mother had been very creative and artistic, crocheting, embroidering and making lace, always giving handmade gifts to visitors and to girls in the neighbourhood who were getting married. Even before my engagement she had begun making things for my future home and gifts for my future husband's family. She made tablecloths, napkins, cushions, pillow cases, sheets, bedding and other decorations. A month before the wedding, I had a special surprise treat. My future husband arranged for us to go to Istanbul for four days to buy clothes and jewellery for the wedding. In the most exclusive boutique in Bakrkye, we bought my wedding dress, veil and tiara, and a suit for him. He bought me a necklace, earrings and a wedding ring all made of white gold with diamonds. I took the opportunity to also buy some gorgeous evening dresses.

I had a traditional wedding, which lasted for three days. On the Thursday afternoon over a hundred women gathered at my mother's house for the 'henna night' – although we didn't actually use any henna. My university friends from Prishtinë were there and they and many others stayed with us as guests. As the bride I was the centre of attention and changed my outfit many times during the evening to show off all my new clothes. In the house all the things that my mother, sister, sister-in-law and I had made were displayed. Decorated pillow cases, sheets, tablecloths, napkins, pyjamas, dresses for me (some bought and some I designed and had specially made), furniture, crockery, lamps, vases and other ornaments were all laid out for show.

The food was traditional Albanian: vegetable soup, salads, vine leaves wrapped around mince and rice, strips of grilled lamb and beef and the mixture of local vegetables called turli. To finish we had baklava: thin crispy strips of sweet pastry with nuts and syrup. After all this we talked, sang songs and danced late into the night.

The next day was my birthday and my soon-to-be husband came to see me in the morning on a quick visit before my mother's house was again opened to visitors. Throughout the day, as is traditional, friends, family and strangers were made welcome. My Aunt Tush, dressed in black as she always was, arrived with her youngest son Sejdi. I wore the traditional Albanian costume of a blouse of white silk under a bright gold waistcoat carefully embroidered with flowers. It was all handmade and beautiful and I sat demurely with my hands folded below my bosom. As guests arrived I would take their hand in mine and touch my face and forehead before releasing. When there was dancing I did not join in but would stand up, stay still and then quietly sit down again when it was finished.

On the day of the wedding my future in-laws, their family and friends arrived in decorated cars to pick me up and I was taken to their family home. Before entering, my mother-in-law offered me a plate of honey. I dipped the tips of my fingers in and reached up to press them against the top of the door frame, to symbolise the sweetness between our families. We spent the afternoon in the house before going to the hotel where our guests had already started arriving: about three hundred friends, family and neighbours of different ethnicities. They started the celebrations when our arrival was announced by the lights being switched on and off. My own family arrived a couple of hours later to complete the party. There was live Turkish and Albanian music; there was eating and drinking and we danced until dawn the next day.

After three months' living in the family home we moved to our own flat in an apartment block near my parents' house. It was a multicultural neighbourhood with good relations and some of the people living in our building were Serbian.

Later that year Tito died in Ljubljana, Slovenia, at the age of eighty-seven and his body was transported around Yugoslavia in his blue train so that people could mourn their loss. The fact is everyone in Yugoslavia was painfully aware of a long history of ethnic division and wondered if we could hold together without Tito. My sister, Sherife, was attuned to the political climate and immediately alert to the danger of uncontrolled Serbian expansionism.

Like most people I got on with life. I had a family to begin, a husband and job and, soon, Fehime would come to live with us. We were among the lucky ones of the world. Our life together had started and continued well. We lived it to the full and now looked forward to a prosperous, successful future. At that time we had no fear of our neighbours. It was not until our first year of house building, 1986, when A Proposal for Hopelessness was leaked by the Serbian government, that I felt my first real shiver of apprehension.

THE KITCHEN PROJECT

For what we call our Kitchen Project we have pulled four of the tables together in the Drop-In.

This is our sixth session together, asylum seekers, refugees and people from the local community. We collect recipes from all our home countries and are planning a recipe book, but the project has already achieved much more than that. All over the world the kitchen is the heart of the home, whether it is in a luxury apartment or a wooden shack. I baked my first cake when I was thirteen and my oldest son first made me a cup of tea when he was only six. As I write I can still smell the cooking in my mother's kitchen. The kitchen experience is one we hold in common.

Together we talk through the preparation of dishes and what we might create for special occasions. From here it is a natural step to family, folklore, culture and, through these things, to current affairs. The project is organised by conFAB in association with the Maryhill Integration Network and tonight, as usual, we are led by the storyteller Julie Dawid, who sits at the head of the group. ConFAB is an organisation of writers based in Glasgow that provides both means and a structure to aid them in the production of high quality work. Only recently they presented a play by Liam Stewart about the lives of asylum seekers. The Flats was performed to full houses and real appreciation, by asylum seekers working with conFAB and members of the host community.

Across from me sits Samira, an Iraqi woman. Samira has a slight, but strong, physique and a likeness to Mother Theresa that is accentuated by the headscarf she wears. Mother Theresa is part of my Albanian Kosovar heritage and I think of her with pride. Her father was from Prizeren and her mother from Novosell, a village near Gkakova, although she was born in Skopje, in Macedonia, and given the name Gongje Bojaxhiu. In later years she said, 'By blood I am Albanian, by citizenship Indian. I belong to the world.'

Samira has been cut off from her homeland by war, living with her brother in Glasgow. 'I am grateful for these evenings,' she says. 'Not so much for recipes and food, but to speak of books and to share our experiences has brought a sort of revival into my life.'

Beside her is Zena, from Libya, who wears a plain, black abaya and black headscarf so that only her face and hands can be seen. On Samira's other side are two older men. Mahmed is from Algeria. He is fluent in several languages but English is not yet one of them. It steadily improves though. I have great respect for his intelligence. The other is Mohammed from Egypt. A broadly built man in corduroy, he has the air of someone who has known some level of authority.

Beside them are three West African women in their early twenties. Two of them are mothers. One is Charlotte, who has a little boy named David, now playing at the top of the hall with Artur. Nuna, Artur's mother, is from Armenia and sits on my other side with an Armenian couple. As far as I know they are not related, but she befriends them and translates for them as required.

Nuna arrived in this country five years ago so I have known her all the time I have worked with the Network. A tremendous contributor, she loves to bake and never lets anyone's birthday go by without a cake. I understood early that she has qualities that set her apart. She is calm and patient and, from her earlier life, brings a dance talent she uses to choreograph the children of asylum seekers and the host community together. I do not ask too much about anyone's former life, even when I am as close to them as I am to Nuna.

Tonight the asylum seekers have spontaneously arranged themselves in groups of likeness. That is to say the older Middle Eastern women have sat together, as have the older North African men and the young West African women, and the Armenians. Community Worker C and Julie are sitting together as well, just as Sharon, our Administration Worker from Donegal, sits close to me. A beautiful, dark-haired young woman, she is possessed of a quiet thoughtfulness in equal measure to her enthusiasm. I am fortunate to have her working with me.

Tonight Julie asks the asylum seekers to provide a short biography that will sit beside their recipes and stories in the book. As in all we do there is no compulsion to participate. Indeed, not all can yet communicate sufficiently well in English. Some have other reasons for remaining silent, some political, some personal. All are casualties of one sort or another.

Zena as usual is quiet. She hands over to Samira who tells us that the Iraqi people did not deserve this war. She speaks of the buildings that have been destroyed and the civilisation that has been compromised by tyranny and conflict. Samira loves to talk. She is well educated and cultured and tries to keep herself informed. In Iraq she was an English teacher. Tonight her emotions rise to the surface and there are a few tears. She passes over to Mohammed from Egypt. At first he does not wish to speak but soon relents. At home he was a politician. We pass on to the West Africans.

Like young women everywhere they have a tendency to

giggle. The first two let the opportunity go past. The third speaks. 'My name is Charlotte and I am from Ivory Coast. While I am here I am studying at Glasgow Caledonian University in computers. I also have a little boy, David.' And she goes on with a confidence that, I believe, has a note of grievance in it, also an element of defiance. Later she will ask Julie what degree she achieved at university.

A Kurdish couple from Iraq now arrive. They have come with sweet foods prepared in the style of their country, dates wrapped in pastry, to be passed around. The Armenian man rises to his feet and speaks haltingly. He is very new to English and his attempt is brave and worth making and, because the will to be patient is present in us all, he is eventually understood.

We have a short break for tea during which Azer from Azerbaijan puts on a tape of his own singing. 'Six languages,' he says. 'I sing in six languages.' He has an outgoing nature and shakes hands with everyone. 'This is a Julio Iglesias song,' he says. Listening to the tape I cannot tell if this really is the voice of Julio Iglesias or whether Azer has sung over it or beside it, or removed it and sung over the backing. His case has failed and he faces deportation. 'Every day I worry that Immigration will come to ask me, "Why are you still here? You have to go home!" Every day!'

During the break we have our photographs taken for the book, first inside as individuals, then outside as a group. The Kitchens Project has been very successful, well attended and enjoyed. Soon we will provide training and assessments which will build on these meetings and, when it all ends, everyone will have a certificate in Food Hygiene. Always constructive, we will involve them, if they wish, in food preparation for future events. We have a Refugee Week celebration coming up at the Community Hall, but that will be too soon.

The break over and photographs taken we return to the group of tables. Roxana, an Indian Muslim, sits in her abaja and headscarf beside Julie. She will not speak of herself and I suspect she is quite shy. She knows about the book I am writing and asks through another asylum seeker how it is going.

'The writing is very intense and difficult,' I tell them. 'Like you I have many painful memories. I would like to talk to some of you and put in your experiences.'

Roxana looks directly at me and asks, 'Why?'

'To show that we are human,' I tell her. 'To open minds and change hearts.'

GRANDMOTHER HAMIDE

When we were small Grandmother Hamide would come round to visit and she would call her grandchildren to her side to tell us stories.

Fine boned and bird like, strengthened and hardened by a life of toil, she would sit in the firelight in her flowing black skirt with her black headscarf framing her face. Young as we were we did not understand how the black she wore was a gesture of grief and remembrance for those who had been killed and those who had disappeared. Her eyes would gleam in the firelight as she spoke, taking us back to a time long gone and detached from our own.

She seemed very ancient to us, although when I was born she must only have been the age I am now. She told us how our family came to be and where our people had come from and why, using blood-chilling stories that might have come out of the Brothers Grimm – the sort of stories where such tales must have had their origins.

We listened with rapt faces looking up at hers and it felt as if the history of our family and our country, what children everywhere think of as the 'olden days', was being written specially for us. We understood instinctively that we were listening to a sort of disguised reality. At the same time these stories made a great bonding with our grandparents and, through them, our heritage, but also served as a warning. They were cultural inoculations such as the old administer to the young without knowing it; knowing only it is their duty to tell.

'I was born in Prapashticë,' she said, 'in the countryside to the east of Prishtinë. This was many, many years ago when the world was a very different place. There were few cars then, few radios, and most of the work was done by hand. Believe me, you young ones have it easy! Horses did the heavy hauling, and roads were just tracks. The mosque was at the heart of the community. Remember, this was before the war, I mean your parents' war, and before Communism arrived.'

She knew conflict from the start. When she was born the weary Ottoman Empire had for long been in retreat. In 1908, in the north, Austria had formally annexed Bosnia and Hercegovina after thirty years of peacekeeping occupation, and the dream of many in Serbia, of the Greater Serbia they had fought and strived for for so long, was denied for their lifetimes – or so it seemed. 'And remember,' she told us, 'then, now, always, the dream of a Greater Serbia is a powerful one for all Serbian people, and Kosova is closest to their hearts.'

In the south, outside Austrian influence, the first Balkan War was fought in 1912 when Turkey was driven back by forces from Serbia, Bulgaria, Greece and Montenegro. Terrible massacres took place as far south as Skopje where whole villages were turned into pillars of fire and the river was filled with headless bodies. In the end, Serbia occupied Kosova and the borderline with Macedonia, Montenegro and, most importantly, Albania was for the first time drawn and recognised. By those means the oldest nation in the Balkans, the Albanians, found itself divided across four new countries with the Albanians of Kosova annexed into Serbia. Serbia, in fact, held the southern Balkans while Austria had control of the north.

On 28 June 1914 the Serb nationalist Gavrilo Princip fired the shots that killed the Archduke Franz Ferdinand and his wife in Sarajevo, only 150 miles from where we children would later sit listening. That July Vienna delivered its famous ultimatum to

Belgrade. It was quickly rejected. Every small country was allied to a larger and the dominos of war fell until, soon, Russia confronted Germany on the side of Serbia. The First World War began and the great powers of the day fought for European and world domination while the Balkans fought over territory and Serbian unification. Great armies slaughtered one another in the fields of France while peasants shot at each other in the Balkan hills for entirely different reasons.

The War was unpopular in Russia and by March 1917 Petrograd was crippled by strikes. The Communist movement had for long felt that Germany was the most likely seat of World Revolution, so Lenin, then in Switzerland, was slow to recognise the significance of developments in his own country. When he moved it was decisive. The German authorities allowed him safe passage across their territory and on 27 March he and his party boarded their train in Zurich. The Soviet Union was on the way.

Hamide was eleven years old when Princip pulled the trigger. The First World War swept back and forward over the family but felt only like an intensifying of the violence that had proceeded since far, far back in time. The Russian Revolution was about to change the world and influence the twentieth century in ways that neither Princip nor Franz Ferdinand could have guessed, nor would its ideology truly impact on Kosova until twenty-seven more years had passed.

But we children wanted to know where our family came from; the olden days could not go far enough back for us. Grandmother Hamide smoothed the creases of her black skirt with her palms and cast her mind back to the stories that she had been told. 'Nowadays Serbian territory curls around Kosova on both the north and west sides like the crook of a huge arm,' she said. 'But, long ago, it was all ruled by the Ottoman Empire.'

For years as the Ottoman Empire declined, Albanian families had been pressed back from both those directions. One such was the Doda family who lived in the city of Nish. In 1876 the Serbian Army made a disastrous attack on the city. Their defeat left the way to Belgrade open and it took Russian intervention to save them. In 1878 they returned and with Austrian aid at last took the city. These events led to what the Serbian historian Milan St. Protic described as 'the most massive migration process in the Balkans in the course of the 19th Century'. Sensitised by history, afraid for their lives, the Dodas were part of it. Thirty-five thousand Albanians died in massacres and in flight through the deep winter cold.

'Remember this,' Grandmother Hamide said. 'The Serbs destroy everything they find that is not of their background. They burn the mosques, the books, the pictures. They destroy the people and eradicate history. Those are things neither the Albanians nor the Turks ever did. All around as you grow you will see Christian churches that have been left untouched since the times of the Byzantine Empire. Even now you can visit the monasteries at Graçanicë and Deçan.'

We must have looked puzzled at this. We could not understand that Graçanicë was built between the fourth and eleventh centuries or that Deçan was rebuilt in 1335, or the significance of such antiquity.

'But, listen,' she said triumphantly. 'Today in Nish there are many people of the surname "Dudic", which is only the name "Doda" as it is spoken in Serbo-Croat. In that sense we are still there.'

The Doda family moved towards Kosova, away from the worst of the violence and towards the concentration of Albanians in the south-west. First they stayed in Banja e

Siarinës, a beautiful spa town with hot springs and geysers, but they found no rest from persecution and so moved on over the mountains until, among the forests and gorges on the west side, they found a place they reckoned would make a good farm. The ground was black and fertile and they were sheltered by hills from the worst of the weather. It also looked also as if it could be defended.

'In those days property was only what you could hold, so they armed themselves and prepared to be strong and here they built.' Grandmother Hamide's eyes became distant and troubled when she remembered her life as a young woman in the mountains around Svircë. 'The Dodas worked hard,' she said, 'but life never became easy. They established flocks of goats and sheep as well as fields of vegetables and cereal crops and of course they had children. The oldest son of my generation was named Emin. He was half guerrilla, half bandit, a Kaçak, very strong and a leader. Whenever something happened in the area it was he the soldiers came in search of.'

From Svircë, Emin fought Germans, Bulgarians and Turks, as well as Serbs, in a confused attrition that had no real beginning and only survival as its end. As a consequence he spent much of his time hiding in the mountains and there he met with a man named Lil Kaçaku. They became good friends and, when the war was over, Lil arranged the marriage of Emin to his cousin, Hamide Çaushi, my grandmother.

They were young by today's standards. Emin was nineteen and Hamide only sixteen when they married. She tended the animals and ploughed the land with the other women. She left us in no doubt, as she spoke, that her life had been difficult and not conducive to happiness.

'My life of outdoor work was hard,' she said, 'but I was young and healthy. My body responded to it and before long I did not even think about it. Long hours of toil in all weathers was my fate.'

Hunted though Emin was, this was a safer place than either Nish or the plains below. Relations with even ordinary Serbian people had worsened greatly after the occupation of 1912. Now, with the World War over, a new Kingdom of Serbs, Croats and Slovenes, the foundation stones of Yugoslavia, had been formed. The people of Kosova resented the imposition of this new state and in those early years refused to serve in the army or pay taxes. Kaçak resistance occurred here and there and yet another round of Serbian atrocities began. Their cannons razed the area around Peja, destroying village after village. Worse than the regular forces were the paramilitary Chetniks that followed them. Bands of thugs and criminals massacred hundreds at Sandzac and hundreds more at Gjakova. Albanian language schools were closed and Serbian settlers sent in to take the places of those who had been cleared.

'My mother, your great-grandmother, remained in Prapashticë with my brothers and sisters,' she said, 'living as peacefully as they could. For most people it was a time to say and do little and remain as invisible as possible against the fear of attack, but terrible rumours passed from mouth to ear. Villages to the north were being attacked and refugees, called the Kaçak, were fleeing south. Some settled close by but they were pursued by soldiers intent on continuing the persecution.'

Hamide's grandparents still lived on the other side of Prishtinë, deep in the area where the worst incidents had occurred. One Saturday in January 1921, when snow lay on the ground, Hamide's mother took her children to visit her own mother in the family home. They were the lucky ones. Next day, the 3rd Serbian Army and their Chetniks surrounded Keqekollë and neighbouring Prapashticë. They believed that refuge had been given to the Kaçak and were intent on taking revenge, what they called 'punishment'.

'Our spiritual leader in Prapashticë at that time was named Mullah Ademi,' said Grandmother Hamide. 'A good man, a wise man, a man of great learning, he had been educated in the madressa in Skopje, away to the south through the mountain passes of Macedonia. Without such a man the town would have no head and all would be confusion.'

On the first day the soldiers entered Mullah Ademi's home in Keqekollë and beheaded thirteen members of his family before his eyes. After this they cut the bodies into pieces and burned them while Mullah Ademi was forced to watch. Only one member of the family survived, an eleven-year-old grandson who was not at home. After this was done they beheaded the Mullah also. They were only the first to die.

'They did no more that day, instead allowing the population to think on what had happened. Can you imagine how frightened the villagers were? How, overnight, they must have wondered what would happen next? On the second day, in Prapashticë, the commanding officer called all the men and boys between the ages of fifteen and fifty-five to the centre of the village.'

He told them to hand over all their weapons immediately and said his soldiers would search the houses. If they anywhere found so much as a bullet, never mind a firearm, he said, they would kill every member of that household. If the men obeyed though, no harm would be done. Others were told to go home and prepare special foods for the soldiers, barbecued dishes, sweet desserts, and so on. In fear for the lives of their families the men did what they were told, brought out all their weapons and handed them over while the soldiers feasted.

'How the Chetniks must have laughed,' Grandmother Hamide said. 'What the villagers did not realise is that this tactic was the Serbian way with massacres. They would divide the people and first of all kill the leaders. Those who might put up a fight would now be confused and easy to isolate and destroy. After that the women and children would be defenceless.

'So, they split the men into groups,' she said, 'tying them together by their belts, and led them off to search the houses. But some of them couldn't even wait for that. They turned on the men before they reached their homes. All the men of fighting age were killed and now their loved ones had no one to defend them.'

The Gjakaj family were taken from their home while the soldiers filled it with hay and set it alight before forcing them back inside. One of the family, no one can know who, tried to save the life of a baby by throwing him through a window. The soldiers threw the poor child back. This was repeated and on the third time the baby was shot and paraded on a bayonet through the streets. Twenty members of the family were burned to death.

Close by, ten members of the Avdullahu family were stabbed. Fourteen members of the Dublaku family were also killed. Others were stabbed or burned alive.

'Ali's son Rashitit had his eyes removed and then his ears. Arguing over the sex of the child one pregnant woman was carrying they slit her across the tummy with their knives, took out the living baby and threw it into the snow.

'But these people had names,' Grandmother Hamide said. 'They had dignity. Remember these people had names. That baby was the Ibrahimit child, or would have been.'

The soldiers went mad. By the day's end one thousand and twenty people had been killed and everything of value stolen. Money, valuables, horses were driven away, cattle, all. Everything the soldiers could not kill or steal was burned.

'When they were done,' she told us, 'Prapashticë was like a giant crematorium. The few who escaped returned after five days to find the remains of babies that had been eaten by dogs, children impaled on garden fences, their neighbours and loved ones left where they were killed, the sights and smells awful. When the survivors had buried their dead and cleaned up, the Serbian government gifted the land to forty-nine families of their own.'

There are very few stories of good to set against the evil, but it is important that they are told. Sadik Bajra was just a boy at the time, lost and terrified among the killing. When he saw a Serbian soldier approach he was paralysed by fear until he felt a hand on his shoulder and heard a voice that said simply, 'Don't be scared.'

When the first soldier grabbed him and tried to impale him on a fencepost the same voice told Sadik to run. The second soldier wrestled with his comrade and pushed him to the ground and Sadik ran and survived. He was the only member of his family to live and no one can know what happened to his saviour.

Later another Serbian, known as Mileta the son of Velkas, gave shelter to a few terrified survivors in the village of Koliqi.

'It took two weeks for the news to reach us in Svircë,' said Grandmother Hamide. 'After the overwhelming horror my first thoughts were for my family, but on the other side of Prishtinë my mother had heard more quickly than I. Already she was taking my brothers and sisters south, escaping to Macedonia and then to Turkey where they remained for the rest of their lives. From the moment word came through of what had happened she knew that she could not return. My father's brother, Qazim Çaushi, with seven members of the family were all killed and burned in the house. I had no close relations left in Kosova except my cousin Lil, and I never saw my mother again.'

Also among the survivors was Grandmother Hamide's cousin, Lil Kaçaku. He would remember these events for all of his life and told them to, among others, the author Ramadan Ibrahimi for his book. I remember him with great affection. He came often to visit us at my parents' home, wearing his white Albanian bonnet and long white beard, bent over his walking stick but with a great memory. He also recounted his stories of Prapashticë to me as direct testimony and with deep emotion.

How terrible, we thought as children, never to return to your own country or see your mother again. Many years later, as an adult, I was to remember and fear both fates for myself.

Grandmother Hamide died when she was still young, only sixty-five, but my recollections of her remain strong. Hers had been a life of danger and unending work, and life in the mountains had made a tough and uncompromising man of her husband. She was a woman who had never known happiness, as her granddaughters would. I can see her now as we watched her from the window, her lean figure walking briskly away from us, into the darkening street and the past, into memory where she remains.

After she died, my great-uncle Zahir Tunç, who had escaped with his mother, remained in contact with Emin's sons. The family in Turkey had decided to change their name from Çaushi to assimilate with the Turkish people. In 1977 his son Ilhan, then aged thirty-seven, travelled from Turkey to visit his family in Kosova. In remembrance of his grandmother, Gjyla, he visited Prapashticë and there told them how much she had missed her daughter, and how sorrowful her life was until she died at almost one hundred years of age. 'Every day she wept,' Ilhan said, 'for the daughter and all the others she left behind. Her handkerchief dripped wet from her tears.'

It had been difficult but the family had prospered in Turkey. Like the Dodas in Svircë they had worked hard and been successful. 'How can you remain,' Uncle Ilhan asked his cousin Afiz, 'when sooner or later you know it will happen again? How can you remain when a safer life is waiting in Turkey?'

'Kosova is Kosova,' said Afiz. 'The old lady did not weep over nothing.'

Thinking of Grandmother Hamide here in Glasgow, I feel a pain in my head, my heart and my soul. Although she related these things to me personally I could not believe such horror. At the same time it was real, and not real. It was like a terrible fiction, somehow on the other side of a veil. These things could happen, had happened, but surely not in our place or time. They were from the worlds of Hitchcock and Grimm. Above all, they could not happen to us.

Because of this, when I tell people now, I understand how they suspect exaggeration and recrimination and wonder where the truth lies. Surely, they say to themselves, human beings cannot act in these ways. Their sanity, like ours as children, they defend by denial.

I have two answers for them. The first is that I was wrong in thinking these events belonged to another world and could not happen in modern times. When once again the veil of story was torn away I was there, a victim and a witness. The second is the book written by Ramadan Ibrahimi, Masakra ne Prapashticë dhe Keqekollë, a carefully researched and referenced work of scholarship. I read it and marked it up often in the dreadful month before we fled Kosova and now, as I write, I have it close by me on my desk.

Without her mother, brothers and sisters, or any hope of seeing them again, Hamide made a new family with Emin. In the beautiful mountain country she gave birth to three sons and two daughters. The first they named Afiz, and he was my father.

CARMEN UNWRAPPED

Tonight we are at the Theatre Royal, attending a rehearsal of Bizet's *Carmen*.

Forty of us fill the front row of the stalls, asylum seekers and refugees, volunteers and members of the host community. By host community I mean the community that we actually live among and that accepts us to a greater or lesser degree and that is the first interface of integration. Mostly the asylum seekers wear western dress, their Sunday best, but among us are two hijabs, one worn by a woman from Iraq, the other by a Pakistani woman. Beside them are people from Iran and Africa and South America.

The rehearsal will take about an hour and is described as 'unwrapped'. It is mostly for the benefit of the understudies but there is no sense of 'second best' among the audience, rather there is a sense of something special. The stage is bare but for a table and two chairs and the singers are in costume.

A man enters and introduces us to the orchestra, who tonight are in casual dress, and talks us through the story. He wears black trousers and a red shirt, probably with reference to Spain where the story takes place. He also tells us about this beautiful Victorian theatre. It was opened in 1875, very close in time to Serbia's storming of Nish and the entry point of my story. All the while my family in the Balkans have been struggling in blood this building has been dedicated to beauty and art and repeatedly sending it out into the world in the hearts of its audiences. I am glad to know this. It means there is hope.

The performers walk through their parts and sing beautifully. Carmen plays Don Jose and Esteban against each other but eventually loses her heart to the bullfighter. Tonight's Carmen comes from Barcelona and is very beautiful. Their hearts lost to her, the boys go mad! As they attack each other with knives the narrator talks them, and us, through the choreography, the placing of their hands, the way Esteban falls to the ground taking Don Jose with him. At the end Don Jose stabs Carmen, as he does at the end of every performance.

I wonder if the performers know that many of their audience have directly experienced this level of violence and worse. As surely as it is repeated on stage it is played out again and again in the world. Down here in the front row everyone enjoys the show. No one has any difficulty in distinguishing performance from reality.

The truest part of Carmen is the simple fact that the performance repeats endlessly, in different countries, through time. Eighteen years after the massacre at Prapashticë the Italian Army advanced north into Kosova from Albania to find Serbian villages in flames and whole families pleading to be rescued. These will have included those forty-nine families that took over Prapashticë, to whatever numbers they might have grown.

After the massacres Serbian authority imposed an umbrella of Serbian law. Those Albanians who threw themselves against it were killed and the rest settled into an eighteen-year accommodation. Then, in the short period between the loss of Serbian authority and the Italian advance the umbrella was removed.

It's not what we do that drives history so much as what we are. Experience, it seems, counts for little. There is no sentence that starts 'In the beginning there was ...' that can be ended sensibly.

OUT OF THE MOUNTAINS

Police Instructor Afiz Zeka of the Yugoslav police sat in his office in Prishtinë, his hand idly running across the three stars on his epaulette.

On his mind was the usual round of domestic and public crime, both petty and large scale, acquisitions and expenditure, relations with military intelligence and the UDBa, Yugoslavia's version of the KGB. All across the Soviet Bloc senior police officers confronted similar work loads. If he had time in his busy working day he might have reflected on how good life was.

He had risen quickly through the ranks, partly because of his native talent but also thanks to the application he had developed in his early life in the mountains. He and his wife, Salihe, had a lovely home bought with a favourable mortgage obtained through the Force. The war years and immediate post-war years had been horrific and had forced some difficult decisions, but it seemed he had made all the correct choices.

They had lost my sister Hevzije to whooping cough in the year I was born, and that cast a dark shadow, but that was three years before and many parents lost children in those days. Grief was no stranger and had to be accommodated. With the birth of my brother, Ahmet, they now had four, all in rude and noisy health.

Afiz must also have been aware of certain changes in the political atmosphere. By now Kosova had regional autonomy within the Yugoslav Republic, although this fell far short of hopes. Although there was less violence under Tito's leadership, the wounds of Albanians had failed to heal and an increasing militancy was in the air. A number of suspected separatists had been arrested and, in 1956, tried and imprisoned for espionage and subversion. They would not be released until 1968. The Revolutionary Movement for Albanian Unity and The People's Movement for the Republic of Kosova had been formed, taking their terminology from the Communist vocabulary of the time and their spirit from its ethos. In these movements were the first stirrings of what would become the Kosova Liberation Army (KLA).

The telephone rang on its rocker, the sort of large black telephone that young people can hardly imagine today. It was the Chief Inspector. 'Come through to my office,' he ordered.

Recently there had been a flurry of communications from Belgrade, so Afiz had been expecting something of the sort. He went through and sat across the desk from his superior officer and listened. 'Orders have come through from the highest level,' he was told. 'We have to round up all the weapons in the area, all the guns, everything the Albanians have been hoarding since the war. I want you to ...'

But Afiz was no longer listening. He remembered his mother's stories of Prapashticë and how the soldiers had confiscated all Albanian weapons before embarking on their slaughter. He had his own memories of Serbian atrocities from the war and its aftermath and he knew that Tito could not live for ever. Now he had the second, great, direction-altering decision of his life to make and very little time to consider.

For the Dodas, the massacres at Prapashticë and Keqekollë had called forth additional vigilance. Emin and most of the other men of the village roamed the hills on foot and on horseback, defending their homes with guns as circumstances demanded. They wore heavy boots and strong trousers with pistols tucked in the waistband, white shirts and waistcoats and draped bandoliers. In time Afiz would join them because it was necessary to be strong in defending the present, but there was also the future to be considered.

Emin had the foresight his grandparents had shown when they left Nish and he implanted and nurtured it in his son. For more generations than they could know life for Albanians had amounted to perpetual wariness and frequent defence. The prospect of an overarching political philosophy that could eliminate division and war held a powerful attraction.

Lenin had died when Afiz was only two and the Georgian, Stalin, had taken over. Before the death there had already been peasant revolts in Russia. That is, revolts by people much like themselves; famine in Ukraine, again endured by people much like themselves; dissent had been suppressed, industry was in ruins and a bloody civil war fought. Under Stalin things were going to get worse, but little was known of all this in Svircë.

His parents had ensured that Afiz had a sound basic education. Multi-lingualism was already the norm. Most of all they ensured that he could read and write and was introduced to the world of ideas. He read the Russian Greats beginning with Tolstoy and running through Gogol, Dostoevski and Chekov; all of them in Serbo-Croat translation. The works of Shakespeare remained close to hand throughout his life. This quality of reading made his power of expression, particularly written expression, strong and, although he could not know it then, this would serve him well in his police career. Clear thinking, articulacy and strong decision-making would separate him from his contemporaries.

Now the forces that shaped Afiz, and through him the shape of our family, were all in place. Reading formed his intellect while the hills shaped his body and the family provided his values. From a condition of permanent threat there grew the hope of Albania reunited under Communism and a peaceful future.

What girl could resist this?

People married young in those days, as they do throughout the world where they work the land, where strong backs and solidarity are survival necessities. Children hold a different significance in a world that contains neither charity nor a providing State so it was normal for married couples to begin their family immediately.

Marriages were arranged by parents and among the relatively small, enclosed communities of Svircë this held an additional value. Ancestral lines could be recited at length, crossing the barriers of what used to be known as 'legitimacy', and any marital connection which also had a blood connection within three generations was considered to be extremely embarrassing. Families that knew and liked one another frequently joined each other. When there was already an attraction between the young people the way would be eased, but it was understood that love grows as it is nurtured.

The Shaiqi family lived in a village only half an hour away on horseback. Afiz and Salihe were married in 1941 when he was nineteen years old and she was just sixteen.

In the same year Germany invaded Serbia and Italy entered Albania, advancing north through Kosova to meet with her Nazi allies. Afiz remained in the mountains, fighting with his father in the Resistance, rather then joining either the Army or the Partisans. In this he was fortunate because within the larger Balkan theatre another collision, a collision of identity and aspiration, was about to take place and it would be played out, essentially, between two men.

Draza Mihailovic, a staff officer in the Yugoslav Army, angered by his government's capitulation, built up an army from tiny beginnings in Western Serbia. Mihailovic's outlook and stance were Serbian rather than Yugoslavian. His army adopted Serbian flags and took a sort of mythic resonance from Serbian memories and symbols, such as the images of their founding monarchs and saints. Much of that resonance of course, came from their long conflict with the Turks and many of them wore the big beards of the Hajduk brigands.

Their aim, beyond liberation, was the establishment of Greater Serbia. That is, a Serbia that includes all the lands around the Fatherland where Serbs had settled, parts of Bosnia-Hercegovina, Croatia, Montenegro and all of Kosova. Kosova was always different. Kosova they saw as intrinsically their own, a jewel that had been cruelly and unjustly taken away in times long past. This psychology was and remains important to many Serbians. These other territories they pursued and possessed by means of settlement. Kosova was a part of them.

Their notions of racial purity were no less fanatic than those of the German Nazis and they killed Jews, Gypsies and Albanians with equal enthusiasm. In the course of the centuries some of the Serbs who had settled in Bosnia and Croatia had converted to Islam and by dint of conversion had removed themselves from the perfect line. They too, the Bosnian Muslims, were sought out and killed.

Where Mihailovic took strength from the past, Marshal Josip Broz, known as Tito, had his eye on the future. He was a Croatian who had fought against Russia in the First World War, been captured and lived through the Revolution. From that unlikely point he joined the Party, joined the Trade Union movement within the new Soviet Union, and rose in prominence. He survived Stalin's purges and lived through the political trials and, after the Axis invasion, returned to Yugoslavia to become Party leader and take the helm of the Partisans.

Far to the south the people of Kosova were more at peace under Italian rule than Serbian. There had been some collaboration on that basis but, for the majority, it was not a comfortable position. Two hundred and eighty one Jews had been taken away, never to return, and if that is only a small proportion of the one and a half million Balkan Jews who were systematically liquidated it stained the Italian presence and laid down a terrible foreboding.

Soon all was confusion as two triangles of identity – nationality and ideology – shifted around and conflicted with one another. The triangle of nationality was Serbian, German, Yugoslav. The triangle of ideology was Nationalist, National Socialist, Communist.

After the German invasion Yugoslavia had essentially disintegrated. This prepared a way for Mihailovic's aim of Greater Serbia but first placed Serbia under German occupation. Therefore his army fought the Germans even as they cleansed the nascent Greater Serbia of 'undesirables': Jews, homosexuals, Gypsies.

At this point Tito and the Partisan Army entered the fray. On the surface it appeared that Mihailovic and Tito were natural allies against the Germans, but the aim of a united Yugoslavia had returned with Tito.

The second triangle, of ideology, now came into play. Mihailovic and his army held the belief that the enclosed nation-state, albeit with expanded borders, was a working unit of governance and management. Overarching this, on the

European stage, Nazism and Communism faced each other with their differing models of military and machine and shared disregard of the individual.

In Serbia proper the conflict settled into a cycle of Partisan attacks on German troops and German revenge on the civilian population. When the German High Command ordered that one hundred hostages be shot for every German soldier killed and fifty for every wounded, and proceeded to carry it out, it suited Tito who gained more recruits with every murderous reprisal. Mihailovic's first duty, as he saw it, was to the Serbian population so even in this basic reading of the conflict there was an unbridgeable abyss.

He also knew that a victorious Tito would make his accommodations with the other Balkan nations, and with the Soviet Union, and Greater Serbia would remain a dream for yet another generation. He considered and decided his long-term aim was better served by alliance with the invader. The Germans had been waiting for this move, having earlier rebuffed just such an offer from the Partisans. With obvious distaste they chose Mihailovic and before long his army was collaborating in the round up of the Balkan Jews. Over eight thousand from Belgrade were killed in early 1942, gassed in specially adapted trucks, or shot, buried in mass graves at Avala a few miles from the city, and in the summer Serbia was pronounced Judenfrei, meaning ethnically cleansed of Jews.

Numerically Mihailovic was weaker since Tito could operate on a broad popular front whereas he had only Serbians at his command. Sensing the shape of the future, in 1943 the Allies shifted the weight of their support to Tito, eventually dropping Mihailovic altogether.

What all this meant for people across the region, nowhere

more than in Kosova, was confusion. Hardship, terror and death seemed like permanent conditions with no end in sight until, in 1943, the Second Anti-Fascist Council for the National Liberation of Yugoslavia, a Communist body, declared the right of the peoples of Yugoslavia to secede or unite with other peoples. Beyond present conflict Tito and Communism offered hope.

In the mountains of Svircë, Afiz was listening.

It is said that every generation in Kosova suffers its visitation from Serbia and now was his generation's time.

Nothing in the course of the war got easier. The Resistance was active against the Italians and Bulgarians as well as the Germans and Serbs. Neither Emin nor Afiz – nor their families – could spend successive nights under any one roof for fear of capture. Both Emin and Afiz, but especially Emin, were hard, uncompromising men who had been bred for strength. It is easy to forget with such men that their aggression has protection at its core. Emin's heart was softened by his first daughter-in-law, this woman who held the future of his family within herself.

She had been raised in true Albanian tradition. Educated in the madressa in her village, she held her religion to be of high value, a secret place in her soul that was a source of emotional security, where she could hold her own hurts and draw strength for her loved ones. In the use of her hands in embroidery, sewing, the making of clothes, she developed her natural patience and care for detail. The unwritten laws of generosity and hospitality were ingrained in her, probably through her mother. Her father was a poet of the oral tradition and an expert storyteller. I suppose she was a peasant, certainly she was a natural mother.

Of course the men in her life grew to love her, and Salihe had great inner strength. Winters were hard and we treasure in the family the memory of her leading Emin's white horse through snow drifts in the mountains as they stayed ahead of the soldiers, the horse's breath across her cheek, the flare of its nostrils and its noble head.

In January 1944 the snows had fallen heavily on the mountains of Svircë and lay over one metre deep. The struggle kept Emin and Afiz, as well as all other men of fighting age, moving from area to area, village to village along the border, never remaining in one place for two nights in succession. Ironically this left their families undefended.

Word arrived in the village that Serbian soldiers in Vrapce had suffered a reverse at the hands of the Resistance and were hungry for revenge. Already they were organising a raid against Svircë. The village quickly organised a Council to discuss what was best to do.

Another family lived four kilometres away, higher in the mountains in a place that was more easily defended. It would not be possible to get word to them in advance but no one doubted they would be given shelter. Some older people and some with very young children looked fearfully at the weather conditions, the deep snow and freezing temperatures. Doubts were expressed. Some said that to stay was certain death. Others said no, the soldiers might be equally daunted by the weather, or pass them by, or change their minds.

In the end they agreed to separate and hope they would meet again. The majority, about one hundred and twenty, stayed. About forty of them packed what food they could carry on their backs and set off up the mountain. Among them were Salihe and Hamide and children as young as one year old.

Salihe, still a young woman, was a lover of horses. She took Emin's great white stallion by the halter on its noble head, feeling its breath across her cheek, to lead him between the trees and, in doing this, became an icon of faithfulness and heroism that has lived in our family for fifty years and more.

It was her duty to groom the beast's mane and its tail and to keep it in trim, but it was also linkage to her distant, endangered husband, who held the horse in high regard and insisted on its well being. Of course it was practical, the horse carried for them, but her ceaseless care was also a token of their growing love and respect.

Among their numbers were an old grandfather and his two grandchildren. One was a twelve-year-old girl, Hana, the other a five-year-old boy, Idriz, who was very distressed and so unfit for the journey his grandfather wrapped him in a woollen rug and carried him on his back.

The forest in winter was bleak and silent, and all they could hear as they walked was the slow crunch crunch of their footsteps. All they could hear, that is, until poor, frightened Idriz began to cry and could not stop. They halted among the trees and falling snow to discuss. There was nothing to be done about the boy, nothing could console him. His sobs would travel for many kilometres through the still air. If the soldiers were about they would certainly hear and, if they heard, come after them. The old people and the very young could not possibly outrun them. No mercy would be shown and they would all be killed.

The grandfather came to a decision. 'It is one life,' he said, 'against the lives of us all. We must leave the boy. If the soldiers do not kill him the cold certainly will, but one or both will kill us all if we remain together.' He looked from face to face. 'I will stay with him.'

Salihe bit her lip and put her hand over the horse's nostrils to keep him quiet. The group looked at each other through a long and profound silence. Recognising the truth in the grandfather's words, all felt a terrible guilt. They waited for someone to move and no one did until little Hana also began to cry.

Without further discussion they redistributed their loads from the weaker among the stronger, picked up both boy and girl and once again set off uphill, risking all their lives in the hope that all might live. They reached safety and were given shelter in the stables and byres, living with the animals and sharing food until it was safe to return. The more experienced suspected how it was they had survived and, when they eventually returned home, were proved correct. The soldiers had satisfied their lust for revenge on those who remained behind. More than one hundred people were killed in the Kosovan mountains in that period. My mother lost two uncles, one killed in the fighting, the other dying later in prison.

The boy who cried was my Uncle Idriz and he lived to become the oldest member of his part of our family. He had much to grieve for, as had they all, and more was to be visited on him in his old age.

In 1945 Svircë was at last mobilised on behalf of Yugoslavia. Two of Afiz's first cousins left and were not seen again. The fighting swept across Montenegro to the Adriatic coast where, at Tivar, the Serbians inflicted another massacre. They turned on their Kosovar fellow soldiers, killing some, burning and beating others unconscious. One thousand seven hundred Albanians in total were killed in the Tivari massacre. One of them was the brother of Tush who, thirty-four years later, would come to my wedding still wearing black, still carrying her loss with her. The brother was called Sejdi and this name she gave to her son in his memory. She was told that he was still alive when they threw him from the cliffs but she knew he could not swim.

Elsewhere in Kosova a pregnant Turkish woman, then unknown to the Doda family, was sitting at home with other women members of her family when Serbian forces burst into the house brandishing guns. They put the women up against the wall and aimed at them, demanding to know where their men were.

Fehime Sherifi did not understand what they were saying, having only the Turkish language. Others present could communicate and somehow convinced the soldiers that they could not tell what they did not know and all of them survived. Later that day her father was not so fortunate. He was one of over a hundred who were taken and executed and Fehime developed a shake in her hand that never left her. In the due course of her pregnancy she gave birth to her second son, who was to become my husband.

The war in Kosova was resolved as it was elsewhere in the Balkans, by the fighting in Russia and in Western Europe. Germany and Nazism failed and fell and Mihailovic fell with them. He was hunted down and tried and eventually shot. It seemed that Tito had won the twin war of ideology and identity on behalf of Communism and Yugoslavia.

Soon he promised Enver Hoxha, the Albanian Communist leader, that Kosova would be ceded to Albania, although not at that time for fear of a Serbian backlash. This promise became public knowledge and it convinced Afiz that he should make the first of his life's two great bold decisions. A new Establishment was forming and he would join it.

It was time for the Dodas to come down out of the mountains.

Although he was well read far beyond his contemporaries, Afiz knew his formal education was deficient. He and Salihe moved to Prishtinë where they worked while Afiz went to school for the first time and took formal qualifications. This done he went to Zagreb and successfully completed his course to become a police instructor. To achieve this though, to create this new life, there was something fundamental and profound he knew he must give up. The name Doda was associated with the mountains, with obduracy and even banditry. To be accepted he felt the need to make a visible shift from his origins and assume, almost, a new identity. He changed their name, his and Salihe's, to that of another branch of the family. They became Afiz and Salihe Zeka, and that was the name my sister Sherife and I changed again when we married.

It would hardly be possible to more thoroughly join a national Establishment than to join the police. Afiz was accepted and his talents quickly recognised. He immediately became a police instructor. As such he had several postings before settling in Prishtinë and there are many stories of his unconventional methods.

When he was in charge of the station at Kaçanik on the Macedonian border some young fellows took to stealing carpets. To lay formal charges would have led to punishment beyond real necessity. Instead he lined them up beside the carpets.

'So you want carpets,' he said. 'Well, you can keep the carpets. I want you to roll them up and strap them on each others' backs.'

They did this.

'Now,' he asked. 'Can you play the drum?'

They looked at each other in puzzlement.

He supplied each with a drum.

'And now you can play the drum through the town so everyone will know you are the stealers of the carpets.'

The result was that the boys were shamed rather than hurt and chose to mend their ways. This was the justice of the mountains.

In 1949, after eight years of marriage and several promotions, Afiz and Salihe were living in Prishtinë and at last my sister Sherife was born. No one can know why it took so long for Salihe to become pregnant except to say that the war years and the years after brought high levels of stress and perhaps her body had its own cautious wisdom.

She had been aware though, of an unfulfilled responsibility and of how many marriages, especially in her place and time, could founder on it. The day Sherife was born, she said, was the happiest of her life. The rest of us followed. Enjoying a level of peace and security no previous generation had known, Sherife would become a head teacher, Ismet a maths teacher, I would be a radio journalist, Ahmet a mechanical engineer and Agim an economist.

This peace and security had been made possible by Tito's management of the Yugoslav nations but now, to my father as he faced his superior across that desk in Police HQ, it was apparent the victory was only skin deep. The order to round up Albanian arms had originated with Aleksander Rankovich. The head of the UDBa was a Greater Serbian who had saturated his service with his countrymen. He was one of Tito's two or three closest associates at the top of the Communist tree and his power was near to absolute. He had used his position and his forces to break strikes and to arrest, torture and imprison opponents. To refuse an order that originated with this man would be an act of tremendous courage, or perhaps foolhardiness.

Police Instructor Zeka, who was also Afiz Doda, son of Emin and Hamide, remembered Prapashticë, Keqekollë and Tivar and refused.

Through his job with the police he had a favourable mortgage and a house that had taken Salihe into another, happy and productive, phase of her life. Here she painted, attended the garden and brought up their children in a lifestyle that would be envied by any woman of that time. Perhaps they were lucky when he was demoted and sent to serve in the Serbian village of Priluzhie. It would be no easy passage for either of them, but at least he was alive and the family remained complete. It meant my mother lost her home and her garden in Prishtinë, but she understood his decision and followed him without complaint.

My father took early retirement from the police after twenty-five years of faithful service, the first possible opportunity. He would not begin another career, but continued to work as a bus inspector and also managed a café.

Before this, in 1960, he had moved the family to Gjilan and, when Emin and Hamide came to live nearby, the family connection with the mountains of Svircë was severed. It was from here we heard of the fall of Rankovich, when investigations into his activities revealed a wide range of corruption that included forced labour by prisoners in the construction of villas for his officials, smuggling and the black market. In fact they were gangsters, as were those who would follow in the wake of Communism.

In 1974 Kosova would become autonomous within Yugoslavia but that would not secure a peaceful existence for long. This had been evident in the second great choice of his life, when Afiz knowingly relinquished his Establishment position. Tito's promise of Albanian unity remained unfulfilled and the Greater Serbian ambition remained. Nothing essential had changed. Not in my father's choice but in his having to make it, the dream of Yugoslavia at peace with itself was laid to rest and Tito's battle for the future lost.

FATHER AND CHILD

This afternoon I have returned to the Drop-In Café below my office.

It is a warm day and I am tired but also a bit disappointed. Earlier I was told there will be no more funding for one of our projects, the Oasis Women's Group. Naturally I had to tell the people involved. They took it with a sort of stoic resignation. When you are as dependent as the asylum seekers you grow accustomed to setback and develop a pessimistic realism.

Tears were shed by the volunteers.

There is nothing more to be done so I will take it easy for a while. I'll drink a cup of tea and take the opportunity to sit on my own at one of the vinyl top tables.

There are one or two others around as well as the volunteer workers in the kitchen. One is a woman who looks as if she has a close acquaintance with alcohol. From behind a wooden screen decorated with tulip shapes there comes the click-click of pool balls as they cannon against one another. Some unemployed men are filling their time. We, all of us, are what this place is for. This hall is used for many things, the Kitchen Project, dance rehearsals, dress making.

As I take the weight off my feet this reverie is disturbed by a high chirruping sound from the other end of the table. Someone I recognise has sat there although I do not know his name. He looks like he might be Iraqi, or possibly Egyptian. He is about thirty, broadly built, and wears an Omar Sharif moustache.

Usually he is with his wife. Not today though. Today he has their baby daughter in a pushchair beside him. It is she he is amusing by chirruping and stroking her cheek. She loves this. When she is laughing heartily Dad opens a caramel wafer and gives it his full attention.

Baby doesn't like this. She starts to cry.

Quickly he finishes the caramel wafer and rolls the wrapper into a tube. He offers it to her and when she reaches out, snatches it away again. The little girl thinks this is great. Her face creases into a big smile and she brings the house down with laughter. Not for long though. When Dad places the tube on her head she starts to cry again.

No wonder.

Dad takes the tube off her head and offers it to her; anything for peace. She grabs it and into her mouth it goes. He takes it out and she starts to cry again. Mum turns up and all is well.

Babies are the same everywhere. Dads too, I guess.

DREAMING OF ALBANIA

Inevitably the calls for independence grew louder; first though, the focus was on institutions.

Did we really understand, I wonder, that the wind of change then blowing across us also blew outside the Soviet Bloc? Relations between parents and young adults had altered into a condition of near equality, at least in the eyes of the young. Better education had proved to be more than merely training for a place in whatever economic model we might live within, Communist or Capitalist. It had brought an opening of minds and a questioning of attitudes.

In Paris the universities and high schools were closed by strikes and, everywhere, the Women's Movement was gathering strength. All across the world people were marching, and so were the Albanian Kosovars. Even in Belgrade, the capital of Serbia, students marched for change. Unlike the Parisians though, the Albanians marched to establish a university, not to close one.

At that time I was twelve, going on thirteen, and my mind was not on politics. I was aware though, of the sound of protest, the cries in the streets, the voices of disaffection. Kosova's economy was controlled by Serbia. In particular, the zinc, lead, gold and silver mines at Trepça fed into the Serbian economy. Kosova had always suffered low government investment and, of course, the effect of a supply economy is that it delivers no local surplus for inward investment and growth.

We had been entirely in the hands of Belgrade, both economically and culturally. Many Albanians left for Turkey because they were allowed neither to practise their religion nor to declare their Albanian heritage. Teachers, in particular, were under constant UDBa surveillance.

We wanted to be a republic, and we wanted a university in Prishtinë. My sister Sherife and brother Ismet joined the marches and I remember how they would return elated by action and the possibility of change. Our father was less enthusiastic. Political confrontation was a reversal of the methods he had chosen after the war. He must have been afraid of a violent government reaction, and to a degree that would overshadow anything seen in Paris.

'I prefer political, intellectual methods,' he said. 'Marches cause trouble.' He was proved correct by events that day in Gjilan when forty young protestors were taken to prison, some of them to be held there for years. He had to agree that, as things stood, we had no real institutions within which to operate intellectually. A step change was required.

As Albanians, we were proud of our education system up to the point where students had to leave for the universities in Belgrade, Zagreb, Paris, Vienna or elsewhere abroad. Our children embarked on primary education at the age of seven after completing as many as four years at nursery level. These four years allowed not only for working parents to continue earning but to ease their children into mainstream education. Secondary education continued to age nineteen with the last two years dedicated, substantially, to job training.

At this time another difference was developing between our Serbian neighbours and ourselves. After the war they had begun to marry later and to restrict themselves to only one or two children. In addition, economic change persuaded many to return to Serbia. Houses had higher value in Kosova. With family connections to the north they could sell up and move profitably. This meant that the small proportion of Serbians in Kosova gradually became smaller.

Our young people would leave secondary school with only rudimentary job training. It was common for young couples to have children more or less immediately once they got married, and of course both new parents had to begin earning to support their new family.

Sherife decided early that she wanted to work in the education system, believing this was where she might best effect beneficial change. For five years in secondary school she trained as a teacher and when she left in 1969, at age twenty, she married Ferat. They left for a month's honeymoon in Split, on the Croatian Adriatic coast.

I was fourteen and Sherife had for years been my shining light. From childhood she had been wise beyond her years, equipped from birth with a far-seeing mind and a penetrating wit. So much so that our mother took to testing her opinion on even important family matters from age thirteen. 'Why not?' Mum would ask. 'She is usually right.'

I could not understand why she should stay away from us for so long. A whole month! I felt quite betrayed.

The protest movement was at least partially successful. Kosova was not yet autonomous, far less a republic, but Prishtinë University was established in 1970. From the outset it was seen as a university primarily for Albanians and it made its linkages with the universities in Tirana, in Albania proper, rather than in Belgrade.

Our brother Ismet was among the first draft of students, enrolling to study Maths in our own, Albanian, language. After completing her teaching qualification, and a further two years to obtain a nursery qualification, Sherife went on to take her own degree on a part-time course at Prishtinë University. She gave birth to her first son, Albert, and three years later to Adonis, on exactly the same date.

'Mum was right about how organised I am,' she told me while she was nursing Adonis. 'I'm saving a fortune on birthday parties!'

Sherife was freer than any woman in our family had ever been. This was not only true in practical terms, but also true in her mind and heart. She was probably the closest to being a wholly independent woman that Kosova had ever seen.

She and Ferat had rented a flat of their own in Gjilan where, with Sherife's practical support, Ferat excelled in his studies and harboured ambitions to continue on a post-graduate course. When I visited their home with our mother we would find Sherife pressing flowers into books for him and logging field work. When his professor told him he was capable of taking his doctorate at the university in Zagreb she unhesitatingly insisted that he continue his studies, but equally insisted in remaining in Gjilan to continue with her own work.

Sherife held enlightened visions for both private family life and the public life of the country that were far ahead of the politicians'. Below the surface the struggle for control continued in such institutions such as the Communist Party, but elsewhere the new freedoms impelled a more progressive agenda.

In the villages around Gjilan, Sherife founded the Women's Cooperative Movement, bringing organisation to the making of craft goods such as Albanian women had always created with their busy hands. Beside those communal village factories though, she also created a selling system that turned the women's efforts into money and advanced them, through the market, into a more progressive and open economy. Then they too were more liberated than ever before, and their relations with their men were altered as they moved out of dependency into something more closely resembling partnership.

Beyond these practicalities she preached a lifestyle that could be, would be, richer and better for both sexes. She said often that she wanted to open men's eyes to a new future with women. 'It is time,' she declared, 'for men no longer to be visitors in their own homes.'

Sherife did not describe herself as a feminist because, like me, she believed in love and the family with Woman and Motherhood as its main supporting pillars. To these visions, by her actions in the wider community and the example she gave with her own family, she dedicated her life.

Behind her, behind us all was the figure of our mother, Salihe. An unfailing well of calm strength, her position was nonetheless one of compromise and patience.

Her Muslim faith and quiet spirituality remained central to her inner life and so influenced us in all we did. However, as the wife of a senior police officer and member of the Communist Party she was obliged to sublimate this part of her being. From the day my father joined the Party she did not go to Mosque. Instead she read the Qur'an regularly in private, and prayed every day. Prayer in fact, was one of her principal means of support for the family.

All of us were aware that she prayed for us, to 'keep us right', as family and as individuals, and none more so than our father. It was he who was the most convinced in his atheism; it was Dad who made the break from vague belief in a far-seeing invisible hand to trust in his own efforts in the here and now. Still, Mum prayed.

I look back on their love for one another from my present

position and see this difference as making no difference.

She approved of Sherife in her marching and her activism and her lifestyle of independence and outreach, but she had the conservatism of a woman whose experience was made in violent times and, of course, consideration of Dad's position in Yugoslav society. So she gave no practical support and remained silent even in her prayers. Many years later I was to see that the Sherife of that time, the young activist and thinker, was also influencing the quiet mother. The early seventies were times of great change and if, as it seemed, the older generation was left behind it was also the case that Salihe, at least, was in preparation for what would come later.

If the establishing of the University in Prishtinë was intended to deflect the movement for change in Kosova it had the opposite effect. Instead the University provided an impetus for the appreciation and development of Albanian culture.

Slowly we had come to realise the damage that Communism had inflicted on the land to the south. Possessed of a corpus of literature and song that stands in the mainstream of European culture, Albania had, by dint of the murderous forces that swept the continent in the early part of the century, been delivered into the hands of a hard line dictator in Enver Hoxha, and lowered to the position of an impoverished Soviet satellite.

First his adherence to Stalin had led to a ruinous collectivisation, then to ideological conflict with Stalin's successor, Nikita Khruschev. The thaw that followed the Cuban Missile crisis elsewhere in the Soviet Bloc instead led to a Chinese-style cultural revolution in Albania. Against the tide of history Hoxha and his cronies had remained true to Stalinist aims and methods and kept the people in poverty, ignorance and fear until, in course of time, a great division occurred and

Albania's education and culture were understood and enjoyed mostly by people in the cities. By reading Albanian books, we had come to believe that the country to the south was a heaven on earth. In this we were misled.

Prishtinë University taught in Albanian except in a few subjects. My course was in electrical engineering in which only the lessons in technical drawing and electrical measurements were carried out in Serbo-Croat. We had hungered for our own culture: now the mechanism was in place for a great flowering of interest and participation. We were dreaming of Albania, but only slowly realising we hungered for the Albania that might have been. Kosova's problems would not be resolved by the regime of that time.

The result of the demonstrations, and of our developing self-consciousness, was to increase pressure for economic, as well as educational and cultural autonomy, and in 1974 Belgrade conceded. With the creation of a new Yugoslav constitution, the brainchild of Tito in his twilight, Kosova became a constituted part of Yugoslavia, but not a republic. That final step was denied because, of course, as a full republic we would have the right to secede.

Autonomy within the Yugoslavian state, for Kosova in the south and Vojvodina in the north, meant voices in the new Chamber of Republics and Provinces that, together with the Federal Assembly and the Federal Chamber, was to be one of the three props of the new constitutional framework.

The constitution had been refashioned by Tito against his own eventual passing. As his powers waned he had understood that he had to create an organisation of compromises among many coexisting identities if the Yugoslav state was to continue functioning. Unfortunately for that ambition the real peacekeeping influence in the post-war years had been his own unique talent for manipulating the leading players and the Republics: at first he operated directly under the umbrella of Soviet authority and later, after his breach with Stalin in 1948, in its close, influential proximity. The infinitely varied Yugoslavia continued to work well, as it had throughout my lifetime, but soon both Tito and the Soviet Union would be gone.

I suppose we had little thought for the other Yugoslav republics. As I said, we were dreaming of Albania. A world of possibility was opening and few looked forward with anything but optimism. Among those few who saw a shadow behind the sun were Sherife and our father, although neither would have moved backwards. They understood that the forces Tito had contained for so long were still there, albeit hidden by the light of optimism, and that the Serbian sense of 'who we are' would never willingly release Kosova.

Conscious of this shadow, Sherife continued with her own modern agenda.

By now she was Assistant Head of Gjilan Primary School and a significant figure in the Women's Movement. Apparently a rebel in her student years, she built on the Establishment foundation our parents had put down and continued in ways they could not have guessed, but that they recognised as within the spirit of the family.

At that time in Yugoslavia we had an organisation known as the Socialist Alliance of Working People. Entirely separate from the Communist Party, but not wholly of the government, it existed as a sort of Think Tank to consider the issues of the day and to discuss them, constitutional matters, social and economic developments, and law and order. It wrote up its debates, commissioned and published papers and was influential with the decision makers of our society and with the government. Its purpose was to involve as many people as possible in political affairs and sound their opinions, and it was said to have 13 million members, most of the adult population. The Alliance travelled around all the cities of Yugoslavia.

Sherife was invited to join at community level and quickly became the delegate for Gjilan and Kosova. This was a source of great pride to the family.

How to describe her at that time? She took great care of her appearance. Indeed, as Assistant Head and mentor she set standards of dress among her teachers. If a teacher came to school setting an inappropriate example, as she would see it, she would not hesitate in taking class while the teacher returned home and changed. Filled with energy, she was a woman who burned with enthusiasm and commitment; who had not, at that time, found her limits; who balanced family, work and political life; who was a model for all the women who knew her and for many men.

In 1980 Tito finally died. In the course of his life he had earned the world's respect for the way he held Yugoslavia together in peace, but there had been little investment in Kosova and our ambitions were Albanian. Just the same, the rule that said every generation in Kosova will have its visitation of violence from Serbia seemed to have ended and, with a relative peace, such things as population levels, education, cultural awareness, cultural development and the modern agenda had developed without caution. But now Tito was gone and, as part of his constitutional compromise, the presidency would travel on a rotational basis around the republics.

In good times disaffection grew and the movement for political separation grew stronger: the insatiable craving for independence. In 1981 demonstrations centred on the University resulted in over two thousand arrests. Round-ups of dissidents continued for months afterwards and even more thousands were sent to jail, some with lengthy sentences, some for months and others for years. Some had to flee the country, including two of Lil Kaçaku's grandsons.

Serbian people, who had been our neighbours, left what was now described as a province in increasing numbers. In Belgrade, particularly on State television, this was presented as a sort of expulsion, an accusation that held no truth but that served to turn the more impressionable section of their population against us. Feelings were intensifying, particularly among Serbian nationalists.

Among the influential characters close to the heart of that movement was Dobrica Cosic, who would later, briefly, become president of the fragmenting Yugoslavia. A Partisan fighter during the war, he had later been expelled from the Communist Party for his outspoken views on Kosova and the direction Yugoslav policy was taking. Since then he had organised the 'Free University' in Belgrade and so won for himself a veneer of academic respectability. In 1984 he prompted the Serbian Academy to discuss various matters including constitutional arrangements. In 1985 they reported and in 1986 their findings were leaked.

The document ever since has been known as the *Memorandum*. It was by no means the first such document. Serbian academics and officials had been producing them about Kosova since 1842, but this one even the newspapers labelled *A Proposal for Hopelessness*. Soon photocopies were in common circulation.

It criticised the constitutional settlement from a Greater Serbian point of view, suggesting the weakening of Serbia was about to provoke a severe backlash. It asserted that the demonstrations of 1981 amounted to a declaration of war on the Serbian people and that Serbians departing Kosova constituted genocide. It referred to a 'physical, moral and psychological reign of terror' that had simply never happened and it described us as 'the Greater Albanian racists, terrorists …'

About this time important political changes were happening in Serbia. Ivan Stambolic became president and his acolyte, Slobodan Milosevic, succeeded him as head of the Serbian Communist Party. Watching on television no one doubted they were the real forces behind the Memorandum or that they would use it to their own ends.

Although still a young woman, Sherife had great presence in debate. Tall and imposing, elegant, she would stride confidently into the chamber and there take out her papers and make the case for her women and for Gjilan and Kosova and for a sense of 'rightness' that I suspect came down to her from our mother. Remembering her at that time I sense a combination of our parents' best characteristics, Dad's strength and intellect along with Mum's patience and moral compass.

She spoke without notes. 'For these several years, we have been told, young Albanian men in the Yugoslav Army have been taking their own lives in unbelievable numbers. What are these mysterious deaths? Are they suicide or murder? All Albanians know that they have been killed.'

She rose behind her desk to make piercing eye contact with her audience and address them in direct simple terms. 'Over one third of the Albanian population of Kosova, of both sexes, have been taken to prison. Most are released without charge. This constitutes ethnic harassment of the native population.'

After our father's demotion other officers had impounded Albanian weapons as he had refused to do. No one was in a better position to answer the accusation of terrorism than Sherife. 'Terrorists?' she exclaimed. 'How can we be terrorists without weapons?'

Her fears for relations with Serbia and their reactions to our demands for independence were already being realised. The times had become dangerous. One day a car drew up beside her in the street. She was bundled inside and taken to be questioned by the UDBa. They held her for hours, questioning over and over again. 'Why are you undermining the State? What organisation is behind you? Tell us the names and we will let you go.'

Of course, there was no organisation. Sherife was her own organisation. There were no names.

When we heard of this we were probably more afraid than Sherife had been. Even Dad could not bring back one of those who had 'disappeared'. Nothing could stop her, though. In Kosova Sherife rose in the debating chamber and fixed her audience with her eyes. 'The appearance of the Memorandum, and the change in the constitution, means this is the beginning of the end,' she said. 'The way has now been prepared for the Serbian Army to visit us in violence as it has done so often before.'

Next day her statement was in all the papers.

REFUGEE WEEK CELEBRATION

Janet Andrews, Secretary of the Maryhill Integration Network, stands behind the microphone and looks out at an audience of many skin colours and languages and styles of dress that fills the auditorium of Maryhill Central Halls.

This Refugee Week Celebration is just one of many such events across Britain. After months of preparation, of costume making and rehearsal, of collaboration with conFAB and the Community Workers, in preparation of the Kitchen Project recipes, we are ready to go. Many present are refugees, others are asylum seekers. Still others are volunteers and well-wishers. The best principles of promoting understanding and appreciation have brought us together, here, tonight. Janet understands all this and gets on with her speech of welcome and hands over to Julie, our compere for the night.

Julie begins the story of the strange, magical stone that turns the unlikeliest of ingredients into good nourishing soup. It is a story that is told, in one form or another, in many different cultures. The very variety of existence speaks of a common response to hunger. She doesn't complete the story, though. Instead she breaks it into instalments that she will use to link the various performances. She uses it to gather our attention and carry us on together.

The first section of her story complete, Julie introduces Samira, another storyteller. Although physically small she uses the microphone well and commands her audience's attention until she is done. Her story, carried with her from her childhood in Iraq, speaks of the stars, and of faith.

Ian Davison, song writer, peace activist and stalwart of our movement, should have been performing tonight with

Charlotte. Today though, Charlotte has been obliged to travel to Liverpool to give evidence in her case. Because asylum seekers have to meet lawyers, and sign at various locations, or might be detained following dawn raids, they can not always be available as they would wish. Tonight Ian plays his guitar and sings his songs on his own.

Julie continues the story of the soup stone but leaves us hanging once again while Sharon comes to the stage wearing a black evening dress. Tonight she speaks in place of a student from Kosova who, after seven years in Glasgow, has at last made her first return visit. So Sharon gives the piece its voice, speaking of the bombs, the paramilitary forces, separation from the men, the fear of being raped in front of members of her family, imprisonment, and the terrible deadness of the soul that arrives when any atrocity might be inflicted on you and there is nothing to be done and no way of escape.

Of course I recognise all of this. I am glad that Julie and her soup stone are there to distract me.

After this, Amel, an asylum seeker from Algeria, acts the soliloquy she has performed so commandingly in Liam Stewart's play *The Flats*. In her home country Amel followed her sisters in studying law, but fell foul of violent political and religious radicals. She brings up their two boys with her husband while they await their status. In her short time here she has become an important activist, creating new links between the asylum seekers and their host community.

Shameem Sultan, from the Glasgow Pakistani community, reads a new poem, *Memory*, and then our multi-cultural women's dance group, led by Maritca and Sharon, appear on stage. Between rehearsals and performance they have been transformed by Nasrin's touch on hair and make-up and together they create a high plateau of cultural fusion with a mix of Gumbo Salsa and Middle-Eastern dance.

As if from nowhere a tiny girl takes centre stage all by herself and beams at the audience. Arzu is seven years of age and she's confident. Dressed in a version of the national dress of Azerbaijan that her mother has put together she waits for the music to start and, when it does, she goes into her dance, all fluttering hand gestures and coy glances. Mum and Dad, Kifayat and Artur, are delighted and have their camera out. A few minutes into the performance the dance group re-enter, the members dressed in their own national costumes, an array of colour and style from Afghanistan, Algeria, Kosova, Turkey and West Africa, and dance around the wee one. No one in the audience can resist this. Every face is wreathed in smiles.

Janet understands the sort of evening we are having together. She tells me there are evenings like it all over Scotland all the time, ceilidhs in church halls, village halls, people's homes. Adults do their turn, children perform their party pieces. It is wholesome and bonding, accepting and warm. Tonight young people from the area have joined us with their rock music. It is good, and sometimes great moments appear from nowhere. Tonight is a fine mix of culture, food, music and company, but there is a soup stone we all bring to the evening, acceptance of each other.

Julie returns and makes another introduction. Mahmood Farzan, an Iranian artist and Asylum Seeker, has written a very fine poem, an important poem we believe, but because of ill health cannot be here to read it. Instead Heather, from West Africa, will read it for him. She opens the folder she carries and, in a voice that grows in confidence and strength as she proceeds, reads Mahmood's poem aloud.

KO-SO-VA! RE-PUB-LIC!

The offices of Radio Gjilan were located on the thirteenth floor of the city's highest building.

We worked in a single, open plan room with one or two individual offices at the side for the Director and his assistants. A good, hard-working group, we were intent on our jobs by day and happy to go home to our families at night. In November 1988 there was still no distinction between Albanians and Serbs, neither in the way we were regarded by the station nor in our relations one with another, but that was about to change.

From the building's many windows we could look out across the sea of Gjilan's red tile roofs. On the low hills to the south I could just make out our building plot and the adjacent hill with its underground army base. Although we continued to live in our flat in town we visited often. The housing development was now substantially complete and a community had formed, as we expected.

Our new home was coming together slowly, but according to plan. By this time the shell was complete and watertight and they were working on the inside, putting in the plumbing, the bathroom and kitchen units and preparing to decorate. Sherife's house was in advance of ours but still taking a long time and she and Ferat also continued to live in their flat close to the city centre.

Sherife's great joy, like our mother's, was the garden, and from the day the builders left she applied to it all the spare time she had. Ferat had taken his PhD and was now lecturing in botany at Prishtinë University, commuting by car every day. Both boys were doing well at school. As they had grown almost to adulthood the trees in the garden, and the roses and other long-lived plants had grown with them.

Planning and dedication and hard work were what she brought to all parts of her life and by now the garden looked as if it was a piece of natural landscape that the builders had been obliged to work carefully around. This she achieved beside her duties to family and to the school and along with her engagements with the Workers Alliance. The Women's Cooperative was by now operating well but suffering from the general downturn that afflicted us all. Many of their goods were sold in Slovenia but that trade had slowed with the deterioration in political relations.

To the north were more hills and the pass the road to Prishtinë ran through, and below us the boulevard we had walked as teenagers, Serbs and Albanians together, Sherife's school, the police station and jail, and the theatre at the heart of our town.

One morning that November I stood at the window looking down at streets teeming with people, all walking purposefully through the cold and rain in the same direction. Out of their homes they came, out of the shops and factories, schools and hospitals, in from Dardana and Vitia and other surrounding villages to funnel through the streets in their hundreds, to eventually take the road through the hills to Prishtinë where they would demonstrate their solidarity with the Trepça miners in their attempt to save the 1974 constitution and salvage peace.

History told the miners the significance of their position. It was, and of course remains, their area that holds the mineral wealth of Kosova and, substantially, of Yugoslavia. Trepça supplied at least half of Yugoslavia's needs in minerals. This was why the invading Germans made a point of annexing the area in 1941, leaving the more agricultural areas of the south to their

Italian allies. To a great extent the history of the Balkans revolved around it.

Of this the miners were acutely aware; in a failing State the eyes of ambitious politicians would naturally turn in their direction.

Slobodan Milosevic had by now established himself as the strongest personality in Serbian politics. Understanding the importance of the media he had positioned his own people in all the senior editorial positions, most importantly in television. He used every means at his command to incite Serbian feelings of grievance and glory. His people organised rallies all around Serbia, supplying free transport to all Serbs who wished to attend and, because they considered Kosova to be part of Serbia, soon we were being passed in the street by coaches flying the Serbian flag and trailing red, white and blue colours.

It was almost as if our neighbours were travelling to a football match, to a World Cup or a European Championship.

The rallies were flag-waving, chanting, truth-proclaiming, truth-claiming events and Milosevic's central message was 'unite Serbia'. No one in Kosova was in any doubt that he meant the old idea of Greater Serbia, least of all my father who had seen it all before, although in slightly different form, nor did Dad have any doubt where it would lead. The strong xenophobic current that had always run through the depths of Serbian politics was again appearing on the surface.

In April of the previous year, in a carefully prepared and stage-managed event, Milosevic had come to listen to a list of alleged grievances presented by Kosova Serbs. While he talked with their representatives in Furshë Kosova, a suburb of Prishtinë and site of their famous battle with the Ottomans,

Serbian demonstrators outside threw stones at the police. Under the revised constitution the police service was autonomous and therefore represented the Albanian authority Milosevic wished to replace. These stones had been trucked in and handed out by the organisers especially for the purpose. When the police attempted to control the riot Milosevic appeared and made a famous speech that would be heard across the world.

In a voice of controlled outrage he said, 'No one should dare to beat you ... you should stay here ... you are oppressed by injustice and humiliation ... enduring a situation with which you are not satisfied ... it should be changed. Yugoslavia and Serbia are not going to give up Kosovo.'

It was all pre-arranged. Belgrade television repeated the clip over and over and Milosevic's image altered and grew large in the minds of all who watched. To some Serbians he was a defending hero, to all others an apparition from the past that cast a shadow across the future. As I was later to learn, many educated, open-minded Serbian people were among the second group.

From this position of strength Milosevic politically wounded his mentor, Ivan Stambolic, and positioned himself to take the presidency. This would not occur until late in 1989 but he was in no hurry, already he held effective control. It took very little time for him to force the resignations of the governments in Vojvodina and Montenegro and replace their leaders with puppets. Then he turned his attention to us.

First he had the Communist Party's Albanian leadership in Kosova removed. Because of the 1974 constitution though, the decision had to be ratified in the province.

In protest, the Trepça miners marched to Party Headquarters in Prishtinë and there they were joined by the people I watched from the Radio Gjilan offices and by thousands more from all across Kosova. The years since 1974 and autonomy had been the most progressive and hopeful in our history. Against the tide of low investment an observable prosperity had been created and, until recently, peaceful coexistence, even friendship, had been established between Albanians and Serbs in a shared homeland.

In our offices and our homes we watched the demonstration on television. The crowd had gathered in many thousands outside the building and had begun a sustained rhythmic chant for its hearts' desire, a free Kosova. Each person raised an arm, pointing with the first two fingers, moving them back and forward with each syllable of the two words that were meant to be heard in distant Belgrade.

'Ko-so-va Re-pub-lic! Ko-so-va Re-pub-lic!'

Inside the building, the Party leadership realised how hopeless the situation was and what the consequences of defying Milosevic were likely to be. Inside the building and out, everyone equally realised that the Party dismissals being protested were only the next in a sequence of moves that would lead to engulfment, possibly destruction.

The chant continued and the people insisted on being heard until the Party leaders, Azem Vllasi, Remzi Kolgeci and Kaçushe Jashari appeared at the door. The poor politicians were hopelessly torn and like the leaders of every occupied authority that ever was, they played for time. With fear in their eyes they appealed to the demonstrators to go home and when they returned to their meeting the sackings were approved.

Milosevic now held the Party in Kosova in his hand, but that was only one step on his way to drawing us into the Serbian State. He wanted to put us in his pocket beside Vojvodina and Montenegro. At the same time this would deliver him the votes he required to formalise the Serbian presidency for him, and secure the Trepça mines within the Greater Serbia he was working towards.

Next, in early 1989, he amended the 1974 constitution and, using his place men in the Party, set up the vote to end our autonomy.

A shudder of horror and resistance ran through us all. Milosevic rallies had been shown on television and we feared the pro-Serbian fervour that had been whipped up. We knew our existence as a people was threatened and our memories were long when it came to Serbian atrocity. In February the brave Trepça miners again led the way. They began a hunger strike in the depths of their mines, demanding 'no retreat from the fundamental principles of the 1974 constitution'.

Immediately the Serbian media, particularly television, mobilised against them. Word was put out that they had food, that they were 'eating bananas down there'. The Milosevic propaganda machine, a remnant of the dying Soviet empire, slandered and insulted them but the miners of the country already had the people's hearts. Far from being alienated from the miners we were insulted with them.

In an expression that was coarse by her careful standards, Sherife described the media as being 'like prostitutes that would do anything for their pimp'. The miners' example sparked more demonstrations, not only in other mines but in the streets and in the factories and schools.

Against the grain of a heartfelt disgust, Sherife was less

worried than most, believing that we would all, somehow, come through. Instead of joining the demonstrations she believed she served our people best by remaining with the children whose parents were on the streets. All through that period she was first into school in the morning and last to leave at night, while she and her staff protected the children and continued with their teaching. Education, she knew, was the most powerful and long-lasting act of resistance possible.

She felt it best that the children did not participate in the marches but could not always prevent this. The only time I ever saw her cry was one night at home. She had witnessed a boy of sixteen, a former pupil, being beaten to death by policemen kicking into him with their heavy boots and, for once, it was too much for her.

By now our communities were hopelessly polarised and people's opinions tended to lie with their sense of identity. Most Serbian Kosovars were in denial of our recent shared past, and very few could look into a future where we could live in peace together. I felt this as a very deep pain, especially when, one day in the office, it became very personal.

My thoughts at this time were never far from the miners on their hunger strike. I was depressed and anxious, so much so I paid less attention to my appearance than usual. I wore very little in the way of cosmetics and my eyes were darkened by sleeplessness and fear for the miners. They had gone for days without food and we feared that the first dead body would appear soon. Every day I went into work – although a stern hand had appeared in the editing of our output. While there it was wise to avoid political discussion and this I did, but my appearance gave me away.

My young Serbian colleague N was one I had taken under my

wing. From her arrival she had found difficulty in fitting in, even with other Serbs, and I had made a point of easing her way. This morning when I arrived at the office after another sleepless night she looked at me and asked sarcastically, 'Poor Remzije, are you grieving for your miners?'

It was a chilling moment and it underlined for me how far we had descended into the dark. N and I had been friends, more than that I had been her mentor, but now Milosevic's poison had reached even her. Evidently she looked forward to the first death as much as I dreaded it. If this was how she was affected how much worse would it be with others, the more hardened followers of Milosevic?

By this time Sherife could no longer contain her need to act. Her feeling for the Trepça miners was as deep as my own. She composed a statement of support for them and for their aims, signing on behalf of the teaching staff and children of the school, and telegraphed this message to their leaders. For this she was demoted from her post as Assistant Head. This was no surprise to her, but she had acted with her eyes open. She knew that if she was removed from administration and authority it would only allow her more time in the classroom and she loved to teach.

Shkëlzen Maliqi, one of our political commentators, wrote of that time, 'The whole of Kosova has risen, desperate, frightened and angry.' This was true, but people did not understand what a master tactician Milosevic was, or the unbelievable extent of his ruthlessness. After eight days of protest, three of his place men in the Kosovan Party resigned and it looked as if we had won. The demonstrations ended and the miners returned to the surface.

Almost immediately the resignations were rescinded and

Azem Vllasi was arrested. The deep anxiety we all felt returned and grew into a frightening tension when the Kosova Assembly was surrounded by tanks. The vote took place at the barrel of a gun and autonomy was ended. A few days later the Serbian parliament confirmed the vote and we were absorbed into Milosevic's empire. Now he not only had the Trepça mines but also all the votes required to complete his bid for the presidency of Serbia, achieving it just a few weeks later. His power over Kosova was absolute and there now began a cold war of exclusion against us.

A programme of replacement was begun among the heads of our institutions. Directors of hospitals, schools and large factories were sacked or demoted and Serbs put in their place. My husband, an international sales manager with a great record, was among those to be made unemployed. His spirit was unbroken though, and he immediately made plans to begin a small business trading in clothing and textiles.

Returning to Kosova and yet another mass rally Milosevic said, 'Serbs in their history have never conquered or exploited others. Through two world wars they have liberated themselves and, when they could, have helped others to liberate themselves.'

Watching on television all of Kosova wondered what would come next.

Although she was aware and troubled by events, the natural development of her family was most pressing on Sherife's mind. By this time her elder son, Albert, had completed his first year at Prishtinë University. For years Ferat had lectured there while she worked in Gjilan and, through all that time, Ferat had commuted daily. Since she had been demoted into a teaching role there were fewer demands of her in school. She felt the balance had altered and it was now she who should travel. They rented a flat close to the University and it was she who now commuted to Gjilan, continuing there with her work at the school and in the Women's Movement.

In fact Albert never entered his second year. He was conscripted into the army, bringing back Sherife's memories of the mysterious suicides she had highlighted in Assembly and campaigned about.

Like me she had been a member of the Communist Party from an early age. Also like me it had no practical significance in her life. So when all Albanians were expelled it held only symbolic value for us as another indicator of what lay ahead. Anxiety increased as we became less able to influence, far less control events. With the loss of autonomy, and the Assembly, and now removal from the Party, we had to face reality with no power to make change.

Events elsewhere in the following year suggested, at first, that there was hope. Slovenia withdrew from the Congress of the League of Communists of Yugoslavia and held free elections. Croatia also held free elections. The Serbian Army attacked both but, after only ten days, and after diplomatic intervention by the European Union, withdrew from Slovenia. Many people outside the Balkans believed it would all be this easy and brief. Thankfully for the Slovenian people they were free. In contrast Croatia had a large Serbian population, many of whom held high positions in the Party, and shared a border.

In answer to the Croatian elections the Serb minority there, with Milosevic behind them, held elections of their own and effectively began the wars.

That part of the Serbian population which maintained a critical attitude towards the political manoeuvres going on in their name was deeply disturbed. Decent, educated people were at last stirred into action beside longer-standing, more political people and students. In support of Serbia's political opposition they took to the streets of Belgrade, agreeing to meet in Republic Square and march on television headquarters.

The police were ready for them and a pitched battle took place. Tear gas and other violent means were used against the stone-throwing crowd but, none the less, the crowd at first prevailed. The police returned, this time in greater numbers and using not only tear gas but water cannon, truncheons, horses and automatic weapons, pistols and, in the end, tanks.

In Kosova we watched on television and, when it was done, my husband and I were left shaking our heads. It was claimed that only one young student, an innocent bystander, was killed. Looking at the level of violence we could hardly believe it.

If this is what they do to their own, we asked, what will they do to us?

It didn't take them long to make a start. Next, our police force was purged of Albanians. In the same month a Serbian curriculum was imposed on the schools. When Albanian teachers objected, including Sherife of course, funding was removed and the teachers were sacked. Twenty-one thousand teaching staff suddenly found themselves out of work. Albanian pupils were instructed only to come into school in the afternoons, effectively limiting their numbers. Only 6000 secondary places were available for about 40,000 primary pupils coming through to secondary. Eventually police officers were positioned to prevent our teachers and pupils entering the buildings.

'If you want to destroy a people,' Sherife said, 'this is the way to do it. Put a stop to education.'

At the University, Ferat was one of sixty-three lecturers and staff who were sacked. The rector was arrested and our precious university that we had campaigned so hard for, from which so much progress had stemmed, was Serbianised in its curriculum, staffing and language. All of this had knock on effects on publishers of school books and the other suppliers, industry and services which existed around education.

Of course all this was intolerable, and in time we would respond with a parallel system of teaching from home. Money would come from outside but the vicious processes of polarisation were complete. Our children were not allowed to walk on the boulevard, or go to the theatre or cinema, or the sports centre. All of these were for Serbian children only. Our own had to find pieces of waste ground to play football on. My own sons had to leave music school and every day some new horror of division and exclusion was visited on us.

For the present though, we had to simply take it, all the time wondering what would happen next. The atmosphere was laden with threat and people began to disappear in ever greater numbers.

On the thirteenth floor of the highest building in Kosova we had to decide how this would be reported. After the Trepça strike had been broken our senior management had been replaced by a new establishment which edited our reportage with great cynicism. Continued alterations were made to our copy to present the changes in a good light and portray resistance as reactionary. We protested and next day were called into the Director's office where we were told to go home and not come back. It was the beginning of the end for all news media in the Albanian language.

I had been at Radio Gjilan since its formation and had put

much hope and belief into its voice as a voice of Kosova. Now that belief was gone and it was a staggering blow. I returned to my desk to tidy up and while I was there a Serbian friend who worked in administration, Zh, approached me.

'Remzija,' she said, 'I am so sorry. All I can do is stamp your health card to ensure you get cover for another six months.'

This she did for all the Albanian workers who were sacked that day. It was a pointless gesture as it turned out, because no health service would be made available to us in future. From this day those who became ill and had no financial resource simply had to suffer. I do not know what became of Zh. Like the soldier who saved little Sadik Bajra in Prapashticë I hope she survived.

MIGRANT
Mahmood Farzan

Remembering
the far cry
calling me,
like the echo of a ripple,
bringing tidings of safety.

Remembering
the sure pair of wings,
offering passage,
and that time
when I broke
losing the pleasure
of open sincerity and contact.

To my remaining loves,
messages of leaving,
'Love is an immortal blessing,
let not busy times make us forgetful.'

Full of preparation
leaving the silky road of the East,
for the chaotic highway of the West.

And now here
familiar, yet stranger.
Kindness to share with the scent of the acacia.
'Here are my gifts,
friendship, hope and laughter,
generous hands,
this heart brimful with love.'

Is there a hand
to join with mine?
To build these bonds,
to offer a smile?

ELUDING CATASTROPHE

On 26 September 1991 I cast my vote that Kosova should become an independent republic.

I did what I had for all my adult life dreamed of doing and never thought possible. The referendum was subversive of Yugoslavian authority, and almost clandestine. No official buildings were used. Instead, votes were cast in people's homes, in back shops, wherever a private place could be organised. In every way it conformed to democratic procedures although, once again, it confirmed the polarising of the Kosovar population along identity lines. The massive 87% of eligible voters who participated represented most of the Albanian population, and the resolve for independence came in at over 99%. Our Serbian neighbours withheld their votes.

The independence referendum, so unanimously supported, was a brave and deliberate act by the Albanian people that took our confrontation with Greater Serbia into the area created by Mahatma Ghandi in India and so ably followed by Martin Luther King in America: that of passive resistance. Knowing this, and with a full heart and the history of my family in mind, in a place I still do not dare to name, I cast my positive vote.

When we were without leadership the man who stepped forward was an amiable intellectual named Ibrahim Rugova. Born in Cerrcë, he studied in Prishtinë and in Paris at the Sorbonne. In those years and later while working as a journalist, he published volumes of poetry, books on literary criticism and history. By the time of the referendum he was professor of Albanian Literature at the University of Prishtinë and Chairman of the Kosova Writers' Union.

He had been active as early as 1981, persuading students to proceed with dialogue, not violence. This was his natural way, but he was also acutely aware of the difference in resource between Serbia and Kosova in their capacity for violence. Soon after the referendum he would write: 'We have nothing to set against the tanks and other modern weaponry in Serbian hands, no chance of successfully resisting the army. In fact the Serbs only wait for a pretext to attack the Albanian people and wipe us out.' In these terms he put the threat to our people before the court of world opinion.

Not everyone agreed and there were many strong voices in favour of violent resistance. To those he replied, 'We believe it is better to do nothing and survive than to be massacred.' These were wise words but it took great character to hold back against such provocation as we were already suffering. Instantly recognisable by the silk scarf he wore and by his bald head and glasses, Rugova was held in great affection by us all, one of those few national leaders who come to be known by their first name.

Filling the vacuum left by the demolished Party and the toothless parliament, the Democratic League for Kosova was established by our writers and philosophers in a tiny café in Prishtinë. Rugova was its first leader with, behind him, the older figure of Fehmi Agani, a professor of sociology. Agani, a man of boundless energy and efficient organisation, became the engine of the party and perfect foil for the laid-back President Rugova. Eventually he would flee the country and, ultimately, be murdered by the Serbian police.

In response to Serbian flag waving and threat, and to some extent in mimicry of it, the forces that would soon become the Kosova Liberation Army were gathering and talking together.

Their following had rapidly increased in numbers and the many voices raised in favour of action grew louder. Crying out for freedom in the streets and in the hills they said, 'We have to give our blood to Kosova.' The drive to liberate ourselves was strong in the hearts of many. Of course it was not only liberation we had to think about: first of all we needed defence, and we had no weapons.

When speaking in London as our president, Rugova said, 'It is easy to take to the streets and head towards suicide, but wisdom lies in eluding catastrophe.' He was speaking not only to foreign diplomats but to all of us at home. He argued persuasively. 'Time,' he said, 'is going to work for the Kosovars.'

At the very least his strategy of delay would buy us time in which to become stronger. Albania had by now thrown off Communism, new democratic movements were in formation and they too acted as ambassadors for Kosova in the wider world.

In Kosova we thought we would be first to be attacked, but Milosevic turned his attention to the republics in the north. Serbian leaders in the neighbouring republics had heard and, mostly, responded to his cry for Greater Serbia.

After attacking, and quickly giving up on, Slovenia, which had few or no Serbs among its population, he invaded Croatia. Serbian forces laid siege to the city of Vukovar and murdered thousands of defenceless prisoners. Like the rest of the world we watched helplessly on television. Unlike most of the world we were unsurprised by the atrocities. They were what history had taught us to expect.

Vukovar was a pretty town on the Danube, only fifty miles or so from Belgrade, and this meant that one of the great crimes of the twentieth century was carried out within easy reach of the cameras and journalists of Belgrade TV News. Serbian artillery pounded the buildings mercilessly. Tanks were sent in to run over vehicles and blast at buildings as the town was systematically levelled street by street. Hundreds of defending soldiers were killed. My husband and I watched, as all non-Serbs within reach of the broadcasts watched, sleepless and distraught. Town and suburbs were battered into submission and at the end the victors were both elated and excited as they took their captives off to neighbouring towns to torture and murder them.

Television brought two new names into our lives: the two principal Chetnik leaders of our time, evil personalities to be added to the long list of twentieth-century mass murderers. The first of them was Zeljko Raznatovich, better known as Arkan, a *nom de guerre* from his earlier life as a gangster. It was only later we learned of his background as an armed robber and killer who was wanted in many European countries. More recently he had been employed as an assassin for the Milosevic regime. A man without conscience, he was now chosen for the implementation of genocide.

The other was Vojislav Sheshel. In comparison to Arkan, Sheshel was almost sophisticated and, probably, much closer to Milosevic. He had been given a seat in the Belgrade parliament where his utterances came to be seen as indicators of coming actions. It took no great insight to read the future from what his speeches and interviews hinted at because he was never wrong.

Arkan and his men were simply killing machines who had been recruited from the jails, shock troops who did their master's bidding and claimed their reward in rape and plunder. Of course they took a name for themselves, Arkanovci, that to some must have held a certain glamour, the glamour of violence. It was the Arkanovci who did the murdering at Vukovar.

Sheshel and Arkan were public figures and there was pride taken, not shame, in what they did. Among the rubble and the bodies, Arkan and Biljana Plavsic, a senior Bosnian Serb politician, were televised shaking hands while she congratulated him and thanked him for the job he had completed so thoroughly. It was only the first such task he would undertake first in Croatia, then Bosnia.

'Oh God,' my father said, looking on. 'This is the stamp of approval they put on the killing of innocent people.'

Later in 1992 Rugova was elected president and a government in exile formed with Bujar Bukoshi as prime minister. Located in Bonn, its main function was to organise finance. The many Albanian exiles created by Serbian exclusion tactics, now living in Germany and Switzerland, were by this time giving 3% of their income to the Bukoshi cabinet and supplying medicines and other support to the Mother Theresa charity.

An unofficial system of education had been set up in people's homes and some of the money raised was used to pay teachers. This went some way to lifting us out of what had become a barter economy. Moving from house to house, teachers met with their pupils where they could, never teaching in the same place for two days running.

People began small businesses from their homes. My husband, still with contacts in the upholstery business, set up for himself in buying and selling. When he had some success the business took over our flat until we hardly had room to move. We wondered how we would cope until my parents stepped in. 'All our chicks have flown,' Dad said, 'and have chicks of their own. We do not need all the available space now. It will be better if it is used.' My husband and brothers moved the business across and soon had use of the entire ground floor. We were working all right, but everyone was much poorer and the atmosphere of anxiety only worsened.

The Yugoslav authorities, essentially the Serbian hierarchy, had looked on the referendum and presidential elections with silent unconcern and allowed them to proceed, to our surprise, relatively peacefully. Of course they, like us, recognised this period as an interregnum.

The Serbian forces were fully occupied in the north and in danger of being overstretched. We had no doubt that, in time, they would turn again to us. In what manner depended on how they fared in those other wars, and in what condition they found us. Again the voices for direct action were raised but still Rugova resisted. The argument to strike immediately would perhaps have had more tactical persuasion if we had been stronger, but we were unarmed. Now, as President Rugova reminded us, and as we accepted, time and world awareness were the essential elements, not immediate force.

The cold war being waged against Kosova continued and we responded by gathering and pooling our courage as best we could, creating a new normality in what were difficult and changing times. Sherife continued with her political involvement while continuing to teach within the parallel system. With Albert conscripted she became even more active in the public field, acutely mindful of her own campaign on army suicides.

Her anxiety for Albert's safety was never far from her mind, as she confided to me often, but she suffered from another anxiety she had been keeping to herself and it was about to alter all our lives.

When it began is impossible to say.

Sherife, who had never visited a doctor in her life, visited a general practitioner in her first year of living in Prishtinë. 'What is it an intelligent Albanian woman like you would have me say?' he asked. 'It is a fatty lump, nothing more. Now go home and get on with life.'

He was Serbian and, although it was in the nature of the times to suspect anything that he might say, Sherife believed him and put her health worries to the back of her mind, well behind all her other worries. I was not so confident and asked her to get a second opinion from someone more reliable.

She refused, taking the doctor's word possibly because she wanted to. Life was very full and there was no room for illness. Nor did we have any history of breast cancer in our family. This particular condition that is feared by all women had not afflicted our mother, Salihe, nor either of our grandmothers or any other relative of whom we knew.

Sherife habitually called me every day and from time to time I would ask her about the lump in her breast. Over the next three years the message never altered. 'It is still there but it hasn't changed in any way, not grown, not moved.' Again and again I asked, always urging a second opinion, until she said abruptly, 'Rema, I am fine, but if you keep asking you are going to make me ill.' So I stopped.

Sherife's attitude to her own health at this time was in marked contrast to her attitude towards others' over the years, but her refusal to act was adamant. Against all reason she refused to countenance the possibility of cancer. I do not understand why, never have, and will take the question with me to the grave.

Albert completed his one year's national service without injury. He returned to his clandestine studies by day and, to make ends meet, took a job in a casino at night. Knowing his mother very well he did not tell her about the casino. When Adonis, who had been studying economics privately, gave up his position to open a beauty shop in the square with his girlfriend there was no reason to remain in Prishtinë.

In the summer of the referendum she and her family went to Greece for a holiday. The whole country was living on its savings but my sister and her husband had held good jobs for many years. They felt the break was necessary and could be afforded out of what they had put away.

Booked for three weeks, they returned after only twelve days. I was busy when Naza, Ahmet's wife, called. 'They have come back early and are at your mother's home. Why not come over before they continue to Prishtinë?'

My mother-in-law was unwell at that time, nearing the end of her days, and I had other demands to meet. As I made my way along the street, later than I would have wished, the old worry came back. Why had they returned so early? But I was very late and they were leaving as I arrived, about to step into their car.

Sherife was lovely in a bright print frock, lightly tanned and healthy looking. In Kosova we have a saying; that good skin is like 'the skin of an onion'. Meaning that it is as smooth and soft as what you find when you peel off the outer layers. This was what Sherife's skin was like that day as she walked towards her car. When she stooped to enter though, her dress opened slightly and I could see how the gland in her right breast was swollen and painful looking. She saw me notice and, as I reached for her arm, said sharply, 'Be quiet, Mum is behind', and was gone. When I called she insisted she was well and that I should not worry.

Not long after that we were told that she and Ferat were going to Slovenia to have him checked for diabetes.

One morning, unknown to us, a car swept through Gjilan, driven by a young friend of Albert's. He was taking Sherife and Ferat to Blacë and the mountain pass that led to Skopje in Macedonia. It turned out she had told her sons of her fears, preparing them for the worst, but given them strict instructions not to tell the rest of the family.

Because there were no cancer treatment facilities in Kosova she had decided to visit Ljubljana in Slovenia to consult specialists there. From Skopje she and Ferat flew first to Austria and from there to Ljubljana, in this way avoiding the air war and the exclusion zone over Croatia. When they returned I once again received a call from my parents' house. Dad had been speaking to Ferat in the garden and naturally asked him about his diabetes. He could not contain himself any longer. 'It's not me,' he said. 'It's Sherife. She has breast cancer.'

At Ljubljana the doctors had made an immediate diagnosis, and also observed that the condition was far developed, too far for surgery. They had given Sherife what would be her first session of chemotherapy and recommended she continue treatment from home. To this first session she reacted badly, running a high temperature and becoming nauseous and unwell and developing an infection.

There was no suitable place to turn for cancer treatment in Kosova; our infrastructure had broken down to too great a degree. The money we had paid into the National Health Service had, of course, disappeared and we were to learn that those who had cancer, or other life-threatening conditions, and had no savings, simply died. Our family was better off than most though, and we were capable of work. Everyone contributed financially while Sherife travelled to Skopje to continue with chemotherapy.

After the first treatments she was allowed to leave the hospital and for the remainder of her three months of visits lived with Ismet and Zana.

To the doctors' surprise she recovered. Although her hair was gone she looked well and was strong. She returned to Ferat and their home in Prishtinë and without hesitation put on the wig she had been given and returned to teaching; for her both a creative act and an act of resistance.

I have thought often about the strength she showed, both in her denial of the condition and then, when it could be denied no longer, in meeting it. I have questioned also how she prepared her sons for the worst but said nothing to the rest of us. Her thoughts and actions were always directed towards the wellbeing of others. Other than that I have no answers.

Those were difficult and changing times as anxiety and grief piled up for us all.

My mother-in-law's health also declined. She had suffered from severe asthma for many years and now, with less access to drugs, it worsened. Without outside work I took to nursing her, speaking with her in the Turkish I had picked up from her over the years while, at the same time, working on the boys' education. For all she and I did our best though, her breathing worsened and she developed sores wherever her weight rested.

About this time my husband's brother fled the country. He had been a reserve officer in the Yugoslav army and, like all of us, was fearfully aware of the high incidence of suicides and fatal accidents among Albanian soldiers serving in the Serb-dominated Yugoslav army. We were asked to believe that young men of eighteen with everything to live for would shoot themselves or jump from trains only days before their homecoming.

When he was called up he decided to sell his home and go and live in Turkey. This he did, and survived, but his loss to Fehime was a great grief from which she never truly recovered. Although she was glad to know he was alive and safe his loss was a sort of death for her. About the same time, and to her great relief, Aunt Tush's Sejdi also left, as did thousands of other young Albanians who refused to join the Serbian army.

I remember my mother-in-law with great love and affection. Fehime and I had some light-hearted moments in those last days. To ease the pain of her sores and prevent further rubbing I took a tyre from a garden barrow and wrapped it in blankets. With this on her bed she could sit in an elevated position in something like comfort. It was a solution with some inbuilt humour that she was first to appreciate, but it worked.

The last two and a half years of her life were spent in bed but, when she died, she left a great void in our lives and, of course, my husband was broken hearted.

Sherife decided that she and her family should spend the rest of their lives in Gjilan in their new home.

With no regular work to go to Sherife set about completing the decoration and, once again, working on the garden. She was undergoing hormone therapy and had put on weight but was otherwise strong and, in no time, the garden looked like it had been given constant attention for years. Of course she was building on her earlier good work from before they left. In those early days back at home she was able to go out and, once again, we grew accustomed to hearing her voice at the door and feeling her strong presence in our lives.

Gradually though, she began to have difficulty climbing the stairs. Where she had managed them with ease she now found herself breathless, her heart racing. She noticed these symptoms for herself and guessed their significance. After contacting her old doctor in Macedonia, she went by herself, telling no one in advance, to have her chest x-rayed. Learning she had water on the lungs she drove directly to the hospital in Prishtinë and the Chest Department to have them drained. Only then did she tell us what had happened. 'It feels like a sack of stones has been lifted from my shoulders,' she said.

Later, a second x-ray showed she had a tumour in her lung. When I visited her in hospital she was very calm but would not discuss the return of the cancer.

By the turn of the year she was again doing well and insisted on organising the family celebration, inviting everyone and doing all the cooking. My husband had only recently lost his mother so we decided that we could not attend, but events conspired to take us there for a while. His sister had suffered a scald and I knew Sherife had a certain specialist ointment that she used. We decided to go to Sherife and ask for some. She was happy to see us, thinking we would stay for the meal. We remained for two hours, enjoying our time together but terribly aware of her condition.

In the New Year Sherife suffered a rapid decline. She returned to hospital for two weeks and I stayed there with her while she had the first of her new sessions of chemotherapy. In that time she still did not speak of her condition. Instead, she took a close interest in a little girl and her mother who shared the ward, and when the mother had to return to the outside world to take care of her other children she continued to engage with the child.

Her hair, which had returned, once again fell out and with this dispiriting event a sense of resignation arrived. When I asked the doctor how things looked he said, 'I am sorry but the cancer is widespread and surgery is not really an option.'

Back in the ward she asked me what we had been talking about and I said to her, 'Oh, it was just talk. Everything will be fine.'

'You are not telling me the truth,' she said. 'I can read it in your face.'

When she went home I went with her and remained there.

All through these anxious and depressing times and although the boys were now well grown, my husband looked after them, forcing himself to be strong after the death of his mother.

Chemotherapy continued with Albert driving through to Macedonia to buy the necessary drugs. At that time, recognising the desperate condition of the country, some Albanian professionals who had left, or been driven away, were returning to work on a voluntary basis, to help as best they could. One such was a young anaesthetist who administered the chemotherapy for Sherife and the two of them grew close, sharing jokes and making as light of her condition as was possible. Staying over at night I looked after her and to the best of my ability assisted her.

Our mother, Salihe, also stayed, as did my nieces Margarita and Arta. That year Ramadan fell in February and we shared that experience together. Non-Muslims will perhaps not understand that the purpose of this festival is solidarity. By not eating or drinking through the daylight hours, and by carefully avoiding gossip and bad feelings towards others, we associate ourselves with those of the world who do not 'have'. This is why it is observed even by secular Muslims.

The spirituality and religious feeling that had distinguished her life put Salihe into a central position among us, if not one of leadership. We were three women together, united in the approach of death, and the feelings we experienced then were very special to us all. It was a sort of return to our shared past, true; but it was also a new communion and one I will draw on for the rest of my life.

Others came and went. A friend had recently had a baby boy who was sleeping all day and keeping her awake at night. When Sherife advised her to bath him at night instead of in the morning I simply stared in amazement that she could think this way at this time.

Dad was not a man to show his emotions and perhaps found it still more difficult because of that. Of course our brothers and their wives and families visited every day, and older relations like our favourite Aunt Sofie. Sofie looked at our mother and decided, rightly, that she must have rest. She insisted that she come home with her and sleep. Mum agreed, but returned the same day.

When Sherife and I were alone she looked at me and said briskly, 'You look more ill than me. Listen, I need you to be strong for my boys after me.' Later she said, 'If our positions were reversed I can't imagine how I would cope.' Then we talked about family, about the past and about our sons, that is to say the future, and when there was nothing more to say I held her swollen hand until I could remain awake no longer.

A week went past and her condition did not change, although I became increasingly anxious. When people arrived I was unable to speak to them, but in the afternoon a neighbour arrived to visit. Her son was in hiding and she wanted to speak to him but was afraid that her phone was tapped. Sherife said to use her phone and was glad when they managed to talk together. These were the things she did as she approached the end, reinforcing her dignity with actions.

Later, in the evening, we were gathered around her, her husband and sons, our mother, Ismet's daughters Margarita and Arta, all of us deeply distressed. I was slumped in my chair with my eyes closed, thinking how terrible it is to see people you love suffering in this way, when I heard her voice, 'Oh, she's sleeping' and then, 'I need a doctor.'

Her breathing became noisy and irregular and we sent for the anaesthetist. Travelling through heavy snow he arrived at about 7pm. 'Sheri,' he asked. 'What's going on?'

'Tonight I am not joking,' she replied.

'I'll give you something for your breathing,' he said, and together we fitted a drip to her arm.

Dad and our brothers arrived, and our uncle, and we sat in silence. Sherife's breathing became faster and I again took her hand as she looked from one face to another without speaking and then closed her eyes and was gone. I couldn't believe it. There should have been more time. I wanted to cry out to God in heaven – that he should let Sherife know how much her dying hurt me – but I couldn't. I distinctly heard her voice in my ear.

'I need you to be strong for my boys.'

VOLUNTARY ACTION

Today I am waiting in my office for Charlotte and her little boy, David, to arrive.

This is Charlotte's day for her guitar lesson from Ian. They will use this office and I will go down to the room beside the Drop-In for a meeting with Sharon and Marititza on the Oasis Women's Group.

We have no good news on this one, not yet. There is still no sign of an alternative funding package. From the start we have been in partnership with the Maryhill Health Project but they have run out of money and are actually paying some of their own people off.

Janet says we cannot let the Group end. It has done great work to bring the women out of their homes, to make friendships and promote mutual support, and to meet and interact with the host community. Fashion shows have came out of the Group, banner making, story-telling. There have been crises before but something has always worked to the good. When we needed help with the crèche Maritca from Columbia stepped forward and filled the gap.

If we allow it to close, says Janet, the dynamic will go and it will be impossible to restart. Of course she is correct, people will drift away, but to keep it going means new financial partnerships and it is my job to put them in place. Today I met with Community Learning and the Refugee Council. Both are supportive in principle and further than that no one can see.

On the positive side, funding has at last come through for my own post and it is secure for another year. This is a great relief as I have been working on an anxious month-to-month basis for far too long.

Suddenly little David with his beaming smile appears around the door. He is carrying a guitar that is almost as big as he is and that he can hardly carry. Not that it is too heavy, it's simply too big for him to handle. He can hardly get his arms around it. Charlotte follows him in and they both sit down, David with the guitar across his knee although he can hardly see over the sound box.

Soon Charlotte is going to begin training for voluntary work with the Citizens Advice Bureau. Voluntary work gives the asylum seekers something useful to do, furthers their understanding of the host community's problems as well as those of other asylum seekers and keeps them in the way of work when they are not allowed gainful employment. Not all are confident enough to do it and, of course, an adequate command of the language is necessary. It provides only a tenuous grip on the future but Charlotte has the necessary qualities and, in addition, is a very determined woman.

Little David lays the guitar flat across his legs and strums at the strings while we speak.

A DETERIORATING SITUATION

The body does not die all at the same time; the brain may function for an hour after the heart stops.

We are careful what we say in that time. Thereafter the body is kept in the house for no more than twenty-four hours. On the night following the death all lights are kept on and, in this way, neighbours informed of what has happened and word goes round. This is how it has been since before we had newspapers or the telephone and it continues as a tradition.

In our culture we move more quickly than is done in the West, although there is no less grief or respect. The day after Sherife died a woman cleric, a hoxhenica, came from the Mosque to wash her and to wrap her in a white sheet, the same sheet she would later in the day be buried in. Coffins are not used except to store the remains as visitors come and go. Most people do not see the coffin since they come to comfort the living, and they would have been unfamiliar to us had it not been that so many of our boys were returned by the Army in them.

So, Sherife was wrapped in white and I was reminded that, on the day before she herself died, Fehime had called me to her and asked what white thing it was that had entered the room. I looked and saw nothing. She insisted and I comforted her as best I could as I fed and nursed her. In contrast to Sherife's, her end had been lingering and slow, but she had met it with equal courage and dignity.

Sherife was buried in a Muslim graveyard in Gjilan and more than a thousand people joined us there. Word had gone round unbelievably quickly and they came from Prishtinë, Prizeren, Rahovec and from cities beyond, people from the Women's

Movement and the Alliance, teachers and former pupils, friends. My mother and I knew we had to be strong, especially for the children, because this is how Sherife would have wanted us to be. Children had been constantly in her mind's eye, their present innocence and their futures and their right to be taught. She would interrupt important conversations to attend to the needs of a single child. We drew great strength from the high regard she had so obviously been held in.

Through the mist of grief the family continued in the ways of our people that had been practised for centuries. The women remain in the house from which their loved one has passed away. The men go into a neighbour's house. Both sexes remain indoors for a week, each receiving visitors of their own sex in groups of ten or twelve. Sometimes the unspoken rules are the most strictly observed. No guests will stay for more than fifteen minutes and each will be offered a small cup of strong, Turkish coffee, nothing more. Meals are provided for people who have travelled any great distance.

For all of this week the family are not allowed to cook, being in mourning. Instead neighbours provide for all their needs. This is the tradition, but after that time it is expected that the mourners will rally and provide for themselves. In the house of the death, my mother, Salihe, was principal mourner.

Other women, aunts, cousins, remained and at the end of that first week we invited all the relatives, old and new neighbours, and many of her colleagues for dinner. Among them was another young woman who came to us to read from the Qur'an. She wore ordinary, everyday clothing but across her head she placed a white scarf decorated with embroidery and hung with tiny ornaments. She read: 'God does not judge you according to your appearance and your wealth but looks into your heart and into your deeds. Whoever believes in God and the Last Day should be good to his neighbours.' After that she imparted the sort of simple, commonsense wisdom that is too easily forgotten. 'You must have patience and respect people,' she said. 'Even when it seems you cannot go on. Whatever happens in life you must have patience and be strong because this is God's order.'

Even then, for Sherife, visitors just kept arriving and there was no question of halting after so short a period. Her doors were open for fully three weeks and I remained in the house for all of that time.

When I returned home my husband switched off the television out of respect and sympathy. I told him to put it back on again. As the political situation deteriorated it became more than normally important for him and the boys to remain informed.

In the north the wars grew more bloody and terrible. The siege of Sarajevo had been going on for almost two years. Differences had opened up between the Serb leaders in Belgrade and those in the Serb areas of Bosnia, but, if anything, this made matters worse. Only a few weeks before, an atrocity had occurred when a mortar shell exploded in the market and killed sixty-eight innocent people.

Arkan's paramilitaries were active, as they had been at Vukovar, forcing thousands of Muslim and Croat women into public buildings, warehouses, schools, anywhere with a large indoor space, to be repeatedly beaten, humiliated and raped. Elsewhere, men, young and old, were tortured and murdered. For mothers of adult children this was the nightmare, but where the Arkanovci went it was also a certainty, that your sons would be killed and your daughters raped.

I left them at the television and went off to the bathroom sobbing. At Sherife's home many tears had been shed but the necessity to be strong had been repeated often, not least by her voice in my head. Now, at last, I was home and on my own and could let go.

It seemed I had come to a point where I could take no more. Always up and about early I found myself waiting for Sherife's morning telephone call. Of course it never came. Thinking of 'what she would have done' was fruitless because it could not be confirmed by a few simple words. It remained always open, and so I needed to walk and sometimes be on my own. Solitude was my survival resource.

Outside our flats there was a communal skip where all our building's residents dumped their rubbish to be removed. As the year wore on and the weather grew hotter it began to attract flies. This provided my excuse. When I asked that it be removed it was taken to a more suitable location about a fifteen minute walk's distance. My neighbours weren't entirely pleased. 'This is quite some job you've given us, Rema,' they would say.

Taking that short walk every morning helped clear my mind and keep me going. Otherwise I had few opportunities and rarely went out. On my way back I would drop into my parents' home and have a few quick words with Mum and, as ever, she saw through me. She noticed how I had not managed to recover from Sherife's death because, in those days, I wore almost entirely black and did not use make-up. My mood had also changed in that, in a manner of speaking, I could not raise my head.

In that time one of my aunts died and I said to Mum, 'So now you have lost a sister too.' She looked at me kindly and replied, 'Yes Rema, but it is much worse to lose a daughter.'

As she said this I realised she was not only referring to Sherife, or Hevzije so long ago, but also to me. I went home with her words in my ear and, not long after, Sherife's words came back to me, the words she spoke on her death bed and, afterwards, apologised for. So far I had focused on her plea for strength, but there had been more.

'You are hurt,' she said. 'You have to make sure of the other people you have to care for. You have to look after those within the doorstep of your own home, your husband, your boys, and my boys too.'

My mother's words had reconnected me with the complete Sherife, the Sherife who did not know self-pity or despair, and made her a living presence again. Our communion of three women had survived beyond death. I heeded this and drew from it, and refocused my life on the here and now.

In December of that year, 1994, the Yugoslav elections were held. Not surprisingly Milosevic, with absolute control of the media and complete domination of his opponents, won. In Kosova we believed it would be wrong to cast our votes in these elections since we had already declared our country an independent republic and President Rugova travelled the world proclaiming our cause. Effectively we were disenfranchised and the Serbian candidates had a free run.

With the support of only a tiny minority of the total franchise Arkan took five seats. We watched his acceptance speech on television. Always smartly turned out, whether in uniform or in civilian clothes, he came across as sane, intelligent, even good looking. What he said carried a sinister sub-text for those who could hear. 'Kosova will no longer be a problem for Yugoslavia,' he told the world.

The world didn't appear to be listening.

I started going out again and began a small business in our flat. At that time there were pyramid schemes of employment where each woman would enlist five or more others to assist in telephone selling. It was doomed to fail but carried the economy along for a time. Working long hours I became exhausted, perhaps more exhausted than good health would allow. We still had savings and, to some extent, were saving again. My family insisted on a holiday with relations by the sea in Turkey. We went for three weeks and felt so much better on our return.

One evening, a week after we came home, we had visitors. When they were leaving and we were outside saying goodbye I experienced what felt like a bee sting on my right breast and, when I ran my hand across, felt a tiny lump. Ten days later it was still there and I knew I should have it checked. I didn't confide to anyone other than my husband. After a couple of months we found a specialist in oncology, a Serb from Belgrade, who was in partnership with a local radiologist. I visited and after an ultrasound check he diagnosed a watery cyst. 'Don't worry,' he said. 'If it's still there in two months, come back.'

Two months later it was larger. When I returned he gave me a thorough examination and told me there was no change.

Another three months passed and it was bigger still. One Sunday I made a favourite meal of the family's, pita with spinach. That is pastry with spinach. I would make it as a pancake for my husband and rolls for the boys. Pastry was a speciality of mine and I took pride in getting it just right. It takes a lot of kneading though, a good deal of work with the hands, and at the end my right arm felt terribly heavy.

Next morning I had to call my husband at his office and ask him to come home immediately. I felt dizzy and weak and had almost collapsed. From Fehime's time we had a blood pressure device at home. We used it and found mine was very high where, always before, it had been rather lower than normal. 'Let's find another doctor,' he said.

In Prishtinë we found another specialist. At that time there was no mammogram in the whole of Kosova so he examined me using ultrasound. He looked carefully at the lump and felt around its edges. 'This doesn't look good,' he said. 'You'll have to have immediate treatment.'

'Oh my God,' I thought, and went through to the bathroom where I would be alone and asked myself the question – why me?

Back outside, a nurse asked me why I had taken it so badly, it had been caught early and there was good reason for optimism. After Sherife I had only one thought in my mind. 'How am I going to tell my Mum?'

In Prishtinë there was another young doctor, a specialist who had returned from abroad, but there would be a three week wait before he could see me. Back home I told my husband and we agreed to keep these developments to ourselves until we saw how the future was taking shape – because it wasn't just Mum who was at the end of her tether. It was also Dad, our boys, Sherife's sons, my brothers. I told my sisters-in-law that I had 'women's problems' and so put them off.

We again travelled north to Prishtinë where the young doctor spoke to me at length. Of course, after Sherife, it was all very familiar. He performed a lumpectomy to remove the tumour from my breast and sent it to lab for testing.

Unconscious as I was during the operation I felt nothing, but by this time I was familiar with the young doctor's voice. While

I was under the anaesthetic I sensed his presence standing over me and even heard him speak. 'This looks bad,' he said as he reached into my body. On the trolley ride back into the chest ward I was already coming round and had begun to cry. The tumour had been of such a size, and so deep seated, that half my breast had been taken away.

They kept me in hospital for three days and my husband visited every day.

'There is going to be another operation,' I told him. My sisters-in-law visited and there was no keeping the secret from them any longer, but I made them promise not to tell my brothers and, even more especially, my parents.

When I got home, very strangely, I felt a sense of release. I put on make-up for the first time since Sherife died and looked again at my appearance. My youngest brother, Agim, visited and said, 'Wow! You look good, I thought this was serious. Let's go out to dinner and celebrate.'

My husband would have preferred to delay but I insisted. I had such a feeling of elation I wanted to dress up and make a real show. This I managed but it was more difficult than I expected; the tape around the dressing was so strong I could hardly move my arm.

After three weeks the phone rang. I had to go through to Prishtinë and see a new doctor. My own young doctor was there as well when I sat down. It was he who started to speak. I interrupted to say, 'Please doctor, there is no need to talk around the subject. I know there is going to be another operation.'

I told him of how I heard his voice while I was under the anaesthetic. This staggered him, but it was true. He told me I was to have a full mastectomy in three weeks' time. The remainder of my right breast was to be taken away. Did I have any questions?

'Can I go home now?' I asked.

In the end they did not only what they had said but also removed a number of glands from under my right arm.

The immediate question was how to deal with my parents. I still did not want to worry them because they had already been through, and lost, so much. Because of the small business my husband was running from their home he met them every day. He felt compromised, so we concocted a white lie. We told them there was a seminar we had to attend and that we would be away for a few weeks. They looked at us strangely but accepted. He insisted we tell my brothers though, and my sisters-in-law, so this time when I awoke after surgery my whole adult family, other than my parents, were gathered around the bed. There were no tears, only a sense of solidarity and love that I felt almost as a physical thing. I asked to become an outpatient for whatever time regular visits were required and Albert insisted we use his flat. There I remained for a week.

The boys visited and I insisted they bring Beta, a puppy Albert had given them. Beta was a livewire and had already built herself into the family. Always curious, she cocked her head at the drain that had been fitted below my arm and risked a sniff and I'm afraid she was quite subdued after that.

Home again there was no choice but to tell my mother since it would be impossible to keep the coming chemotherapy secret from her. She took it the most steadily of us all. She had guessed something was in the air and had braced herself and, as ever, her strength amazed me.

A month passed before the surgeons decided I was strong enough to begin chemotherapy. 'The nature of the drugs to be used and their quantities have to be assessed,' I was told. 'The next step you will have to take for yourselves.'

Through an old friend my husband arranged to meet with a specialist and in fact we saw four, all paid privately from our diminishing savings. In the end, if I was to have further treatment, such as chemotherapy, we had no choice but to go to Belgrade, capital of Serbia and the seat of power of Slobodan Milosevic.

All through this time we had been aware of the wider political scene, not only in Kosova but in the whole of the old Yugoslav state through its slow collapse and disintegration. The European Union and the United States had both applied extensive diplomacy but seemed only to have shifted the momentum of the slaughter in the north, here and there deferred it, rather than brought it to a halt. The Organisation for Security and Co-operation in Europe (OSCE) was set up in Kosova to monitor border activities and looked for people to assist them. My brothers Agim and Ahmet, as well as our cousin Afërdita, joined.

In May 1995 NATO had turned to violence in the hope of ending violence, using terms such as 'surgical strikes'. In this they underestimated the cunning of the Serbian commanders and their determination. They also underestimated the power of men on the ground when faced with machines in the air. The Serbs took hundreds of UN peacekeepers hostage and kept them in target areas. The air strikes ended. Soon after, the Serbs attacked the border town of Srebrenica under their most effective and evil commander, Ratko Mladic. The town fell quickly and the UN peacekeepers were once again humiliated.

Like the rest of the world, we watched the events that were to sicken public opinion in the West and, probably, given the obstinacy of Slobodan Milosevic, make the bombing of innocent and guilty Serbs alike inevitable. Film taken at the time shows the sadistic pleasure Mladic took in the slaughter of more than eight thousand Muslim men and boys. Everyone has seen his laughing confrontation with the helpless Dutch commander of the UN peacekeepers, and most people know of his ritual slaughter of a pig, anticipating the human deaths to follow. The massacres were so well organised they amounted to industrialised killing. The mass graves have been mapped by satellite. Inevitably, Arkan and his blood-spattered followers were there.

Later, Judge Fouad Riad at the International Criminal Tribunal for the Former Yugoslavia would say of these events, 'These are truly scenes from Hell, written on the darkest pages of human history.'

What Judge Riad did not allude to is what all Albanians know, that the killings were not isolated in time, nor a mere consequence of the Soviet Empire's end, nor the bonfire of Tito's vision, nor an episode in European history, nor any other kind of isolated episode, but the continuance of a stain in humankind that has its beginnings no one knows where or when or how.

It would be irresponsible to name them.

In Belgrade my doctor was a woman. We spoke across her desk and because I had so much experience with Sherife, and I had by now read as much as I could on the subject of cancer, she took me for another doctor. In the week we remained there we became friends and she introduced us to her husband, a cancer specialist of such eminence that he lectured throughout the world. We went to their home as guests and ate with them there, and we went to a famous riverside restaurant in Belgrade city centre.

Surprisingly, we had much in common. We talked about culture, about current affairs in the wider world and about politics nearer to home. Soon we knew for certain we were in the presence of good people who were definitely Serbian but also citizens of the world. They were deeply opposed to the politics of Slobodan Milosevic and his followers. Their commitment was to good health, and to whatever is humane.

At this time, as always, my husband was my great strength and confidant as well as best friend. In a sense I had given up on life. I watched our savings dwindle and had little or no belief that I would come through. After I was gone, I reasoned, he and the boys would need whatever money we had to survive, perhaps even to escape. The way things were going the likelihood was that they would have nothing, no mother or wife, and no financial resource.

In the restaurant I said as much, but he would have no part of such thinking. 'Is there anywhere we can go, anything at all we can do that will increase Remzije's chances?' he asked.

The man said, 'Perhaps – there is a drug that was used in France to prolong the life of President Mitterrand. I'll try.'

There and back at home I began a 45-day course of injections around the operation wound and also began my chemotherapy course. My older boys had to be told but I tried to keep it from the youngest who was then only eleven. Neither my husband nor I believed he was ready, but one day when I was cleaning the bathroom, when I was bending over, he saw how my hair had thinned on top. Perhaps I should have told him then, but I couldn't. Instead I made up some story and we continued.

With Sherife as my example I managed some humour.

At that time there was simply no opportunity to acquire a prosthetic breast in Kosova so I used a pair of rolled up tights tucked into my bra. When I was about to begin a particular chemotherapy session a nurse picked them up from the table and casually tossed them in the bin. I said, 'Hey, first you throw my real breast in the bin, now this. What hope is there for my figure?' Another time my dentist, who was himself bald, sympathised with my hair loss. 'Don't worry about me,' I told him. 'My hair will grow back, yours ...'

There is something else I wish to record although I understand it is a common experience among cancer sufferers. In Belgrade, at a time when I was feeling, not without reason, sorry for myself, I passed the children's ward and glanced in and it went to my heart to see those suffering children. Like so many before me I felt I could let my own hopes go if even only one those children could survive, but this is not a choice that we are given to make. We must do our good more directly, over long periods of time and in ways we perhaps would not believe if we could see them in advance.

In the course of the next year I suffered a painful infection of the mouth, the chemotherapy having reduced my natural defences. It had also given me a deep-seated nausea and, with great regret and even tears, I had to ask the boys to find a new home for Beta. I just could not live with the smell of dog although I continued to love her. Facing this as they did, and accepting, I felt later was an important step in their growing up. They were very brave.

After a year two more small lumps appeared under my arm. They were removed under a local anaesthetic and proved to be benign. No one who has had cancer is ever completely safe, but it looked like I would survive after all.

Life was changing rapidly. While most of our attention had been on my condition, we also had an eye on the deteriorating situation in Kosova. There had been atrocities, battles between the KLA and what was now, effectively, a Serbian police force. People were being displaced from their homes. The situation had grown much worse, but I will return to this later.

For now we had to accept that our financial situation was not as it had been. The boys were growing bigger. People we loved were gone. Fehime's condition, as well as my own, had kept us rooted. We possessed two houses that we could not afford. Nor did we require both. Our house on the hill was by now substantially complete. Flooring had to go down, plumbing go in, but we could do these things from within so long as it was watertight. We sold our flat in the centre of Gjilan and moved in August 1998.

People love life; they struggle to survive against all sensible hope. Sometimes it comes off, sometimes not. We entered our new home, begun so long before in the same Gjilan, the same Kosova, but in what seemed like a different world. Once again I held my youngest son's hand. Once again my husband stood beside our older sons, although by now they were growing into fine young men.

In the shadow of the coming holocaust we began to rebuild our lives.

THE LINCOLN STAR

Today is a beautiful sunlit day at the end of Refugee Week and I have returned to Lincoln Avenue for the opening of the Garden Project.

These six towers of high rise flats are home to an important part of the host community, the section that comes into closest contact with the asylum seekers and that has desperate problems of its own. The residents here need no lessons in deprivation or the culture of negation that attaches to it, drugs, alcohol, violence ... but today is a fine day, and spirits are high among the crowd now gathering in the forecourt.

I worked at these high flats for two years and so have friends here and have today been met with hugs. On the wall behind the small patch of garden is the mosaic mural we created with an Albanian artist, a Glasgow resident who has been in the city for five years but is still waiting for his case to be decided. Inside, in the community rooms, is an exhibition of smaller mosaics made, like the wall mosaic, by Scottish and international residents working together.

Our purpose was to bring out the positive in people, to help them realise their talents, and we got results. We were a team. Anna had been educated at Oxford University but wanted, even needed, to work here. Anne Marie was a tireless member of the host community and had been working to its benefit for years. Our meetings were exceptionally short. It was as if we could read each others' minds.

We had fun together too. When we arranged a music night for some of the asylum seekers we asked Ian Davison to provide the artists. The audience was mostly made up of Turkish Kurds – Muslims. There was a last minute change in the programme and, unaware of the ethnic and religious contrast, Ian called in a five member, close harmony, Christian Gospel group who had escaped their persecutors in the Congo. Audience and performers looked at each other with astonishment but, in the end, the result was not ethno-religious mayhem but a glorious conga danced together round the Community Hall, out of the building and round the gardens.

The Lady Provost of Glasgow is due to arrive shortly and a ribbon has been stretched along the wall mosaic for her to cut once she has made her speech. Using the time available as best they can, residents work in the flower beds, involving the children as much as possible. Beyond immediate enjoyment of course, we all hope they will value their environment the more as they grow. There is a strong culture of vandalism in the area.

A small plaque at one end of the wall mosaic catches my eye as it always does. One day as I was getting ready to leave home for work the phone rang. It was Anna and she was in tears. She had just learned that Anne Marie had taken her own life. I couldn't believe it.

Everyone was shocked and for a time things were different. A book of remembrance was opened and a man known only as 'Jonto' inscribed a poem for Anne Marie, *The Lincoln Star*. Later it was copied from the book and inscribed on the plaque and fixed to the wall.

Again and again my eye goes to it and I ask myself, 'Should we have seen this coming?' Anne Marie was an ever-present support for me and for others. Was there something we could have done?

Time passed and life in Lincoln Avenue returned to what is seen as normal.

THE LINCOLN STAR

You were second mother to many a Lincoln Kid,
You helped so many people, by doing what you did,
You never looked for gratitude, you never asked for praise,
You were a rock to others in so many ways,
We'll miss you much Anne Marie, more than words can write,
We'll miss you in the morning, afternoon and night.
You took us at face value, any colour or creed,
You took our problems on board and helped so many in need.
A pillar of our community, that is what you are,
You even watch us every night as now you are a star.

Now the Lady Provost has arrived. She steps out of her chauffeur-driven limousine and adjusts her chain of office and joins me to watch the fire jugglers. We get to talking and she shows a knowledgeable interest in the work being done here. Like Anna, like me, like the residents, most of all like Anne Marie, she understands the work is endless.

BEAUTIFUL HOUSE, WHITE HOUSE

From his earliest years my youngest son was wild for animals.

Because of him we shared our home with a succession of dogs, tortoises, tanks of fish, a cockatoo, even a rabbit that lived on the veranda. He judged people by how they behaved to animals. 'If they are cruel to them,' he asked, 'what must they be like to other people?'

Naturally we indulged him as best we could. Although money was short in those final years we bought for him whenever possible. In the flat, before Beta, the puppy Albert gave us, he had a small white dog that he loved to walk. We bought him a new collar and lead and off the two of them proudly went. That very day he came back with just the collar and lead in his hand and no dog. We asked him what had happened.

'The police stopped me in the streets,' he said. 'They picked up the dog and said how nice he looks and they would take him for themselves. I told them he is our dog and not for sale but they did not ask if they could buy him. They said they were going to take him anyway. I said the collar and lead are new and I would be in trouble if I came back without them.'

I held him in my arms glad they had taken just the dog.

Terrible things were happening every day. One day my middle son, then about eleven, was out with a friend when they came across a group of young Serbs who were celebrating a wedding by shooting guns wildly in the air. They carried guns openly at that time, and shots were fired, for one reason or another, every day. One of them emptied his automatic rifle and after a couple of minutes an Albanian man appeared on the balcony of a five-storey building close by. He was screaming and crying and, at first, the boys thought he had gone mad.

Perhaps he had. One of the bullets had entered his home and struck his wife. Very shortly afterwards the woman was brought down on a stretcher having suffered a terrible head wound. The sight made an impression on my son that will never leave him. She was taken to hospital where she later died, but no one was ever brought to justice because, by this time, we had become something other than human in the Serbian world view. During another such wedding celebration a bullet narrowly missed my youngest son.

Ismet and Zana had begun a small business at home where they made socks, hats, baby clothes and other small items. At the same time Ismet was working as a volunteer teacher at night in the parallel education system. It was because of his work as a teacher that the police arrested him and questioned him at the station. Their questions were much like the questions used on Sherife much earlier, 'Who is behind this? Who is paying you?' As with Sherife, no one was behind him and no one was paying him. What had happened was that the Albanian people had spontaneously rallied to preserve their institutions, particularly education. Such organisation as was possible followed that movement.

As with my youngest son's encounter with the police we felt lucky. Human Rights Watch was later to report, 'In a state where the judiciary has been robbed of its independence, defendants are routinely convicted solely on "confessions" signed after prolonged torture.'

Early in 1997 there was a car bomb attempt on the life of the Serbian rector of Prishtinë University. Many thought it was the work of the KLA, and indeed such a claim was made, but we expected it was more likely the Serbian forces themselves in a further attempt to demonise us and provoke reaction among their own people – and a following reaction from us.

At this time young Albanians who had previously been forced out of the country were returning with the intention of putting up a fight. Others, in America and elsewhere, responded to the organisation Homeland Calling, which was based in Switzerland, raising money to fund their returns. Many gathered south of the border, in Albania and, in addition, young men who left Kosova for safety there were met at the border by former soldiers of the Yugoslav army who acted as recruiting officers. Some Albanians also joined.

The KLA was still relatively weak though, and a truly effective defence was more likely to come from the UN or NATO. The Conference on Security and Co-operation in Europe had been monitoring events for most of the decade but their resources were small and by far the greatest part of the world's attention was on the wars in the north.

My brothers Ahmet and Agim worked for the OSCE, as did my cousin Afërdita, Shemsi's sister. Ahmet, the mechanical engineer, drove and repaired vehicles for them and Agim, the economist, rose to be a senior manager. Afërdita was an interpreter. All of them were to remain in Kosova through the coming conflict, Afërdita continuing as an interpreter and, eventually, becoming Secretary to the KFOR police. With KFOR she was among the first to enter a police station after the Serbian retreat. There she found blood on the walls, blood staining the carpets, and discarded, blood-soaked clothing. On a notice board she also found a list of activists to be liquidated and their photographs with, among them, her own and my brothers' names. In those years we knew little of what happened in police stations but correctly guessed. It was of a piece with our everyday experience.

Two others of my cousins were killed in the army. For one of them the family received a letter two days before he was due to be released. It said he had lost his life in a traffic accident, no more than that.

One night we looked from our window and saw that a lorry was drawn up in the square and that guns were being handed out to our Serbian neighbours. Albanians, of course, had long since been stripped of all weapons. We felt increasingly defenceless.

The tension rose and we existed in a condition of extreme day-after-day anxiety. On the one hand we nurtured hope, and our parallel education system demonstrated our belief that a future would come for Kosovar Albanians. We hoped that relief would arrive from the international community, which, at that time and in spite of all President Rugova's best efforts and those of the OSCE, barely knew we existed. On the other hand the governments of that same international community continued to insist that we were and should remain a province of Serbia.

Beyond survival our aim was independence. Set against our faint hopes was the acidic contempt of our neighbours, everyday murder, and the centuries-long attrition that common sense and experience would not allow us to forget. The situation grew so bad that one day I felt I could not travel for radiotherapy. I wanted to call my doctor in Belgrade to tell him but our phone line had been cut. What could I do when the call simply had to be made? The decision was so obvious I made it without real consideration. Our immediate neighbours of many years were Serbian. We had never been close, but we had always been helpful to each other. The woman of the house invited me in and left me in the hall while she spoke to her husband.

While I waited the door closed behind me and there, leaning against the jamb, were four automatic rifles, one for each member of the family. When she returned she saw that I had seen but agreed that I could call and, of course, my doctor understood. Tacitly, without mentioning them, my neighbour and I agreed not to speak of the guns and I have no idea what pressure was brought to bear on her to accept them, or at what point she might have had no choice but to use them.

For some time the KLA had been growing stronger and becoming more organised. Some volunteers had survived massacres in Drenica, others who had no direct experience of the persecution were far-seeing educated people. Many who had deserted the Yugoslav Army and dispersed abroad now returned to defend Kosova. Detached from any line of command to the president, or the cabinet in Bonn, the KLA nonetheless was loyal to them.

Adem Jashari was a hero to many Albanians but I had never heard of him before both he and his home village of Prekaz i Ultë, in the Drenica valley, were wiped out. He was one of the first to recruit KLA members and would later be described as the 'father of the KLA'.

The Jasharis were guerrilla fighters who had attacked units of the police and were a thorn in their flesh through what was now, quite openly, an occupation. Adem's greatest significance, though, was as a symbolic character. On one occasion the police attacked his home but were outfought, driven away and humiliated. He was seen by many as a man who would never give up, an undying spirit representing freedom, and the young men who were returning were inspired by him. This gave him a significance far beyond the effects of his actions.

On Saturday 28 February 1998 a battle broke out in the village of Likoshan between the police and a number of KLA men including Adem Jashari. When the KLA escaped, the police took their spite out on two nearby households, murdering twenty-six innocent people including women and children. Then they moved again against Prekaz i Ultë, stationing themselves on the hill above the village. On 5 March, no doubt having learned from their earlier painful experience, they attacked using a combination of artillery and ground soldiers. The Jasharis refused to surrender, knowing they would be murdered anyway and in the end fifty-eight people were killed, again including women and children. Adem was among them.

These details were not known to us at the time in Gjilan, but we were immediately aware of a change in atmosphere. News of the catastrophe went round almost instantly and people left the streets to wait in their homes for whatever might happen next. Bad as the situation had been it was now much worse. Graffiti appeared on the walls boasting about the killings. Young Serbians, boys we had known, came back firing their guns in celebration and we felt as they must have felt in the Warsaw Ghetto, surrounded and waiting.

The war had come to us, into our city and our homes.

The killing of Adem Jashari and his family had another effect that would have great influence over the coming period. Funds that had been donated from abroad to the president's cabinet in exile were increasingly diverted to 'Homeland Calling'. In breach of President Rugova's wishes arms were purchased and distributed to the KLA and the conflict intensified.

As a family we continued to follow events as best we could

through the broadcast media. Radio 21 was formed abroad to specialise in giving truthful information about Kosova. We also received television from Albania and elsewhere and were as aware, probably as anyone in the world, of international diplomacy. The wars in the north were now over, at least for the present, and Serbian attention was at last focused on us.

We were tremendously impressed by British Foreign Secretary Robin Cook with his direct approach to Milosevic. As the violence against us increased he flew to Belgrade to promote diplomatic means in a very public display of diplomacy. While he was there the attack on Prekaz i Ultë took place and he returned with empty hands and with, it seemed, Milosevic's laughter in his ears. Some commentators said he had been humiliated, but not those of us watching in Kosova. We recognised him as a strong figure in one of the most powerful nations in the world and felt that Milosevic's arrogance would eventually rebound.

We also hoped that the concentrated diplomatic effort, of which Cook's visit was the most visible part, and the attention of the world's media would prevent any great worsening of the situation. We were cruelly disappointed.

News came in about fighting, disappearances, further atrocities. In July the Serbs took the village of Rahoveac only about sixty kilometres from us, their paramilitaries wearing red bandannas for identification. Arkanovci! Men and women were separated. As usual they killed off leaders, then men of fighting age. We heard later they had transported the bodies back up into Serbia to be buried in mass graves far from the scene of the crime.

The surviving women were told to 'go to Albania where you belong', echoing the voice of Sheshel in the televised Serbian parliament. Contemptuous, provocative, he had said in his speech to the Albanians, addressing us directly, 'you have to leave your homes and flee'.

Kosova is bounded by Serbia and Montenegro, by Albania and by Macedonia. Montenegro at that time was as one with Serbia, and the Albanian border had been mined and was too dangerous to travel. In houses, at private gatherings, in improvised classes and workplaces the talk was always the same. 'Will the world act before the sky descends?' No one wanted to leave but some saw further than others. 'Where will we run to, and when?'

The Macedonian government in Skopje knew how serious the situation was and anticipated a rush of refugees at some point. They announced, 'Macedonia is willing to be a corridor for Albanians who are forced to flee.'

In fact people were already displaced. The number of internal refugees usually accepted for that time is two hundred thousand although it is an impossible figure to verify. Still holding onto the hope of international intervention, they were reluctant to leave the country. Instead they took refuge in the mountains, in the forests, wherever they could find cover. Long columns travelled southwards to seek refuge in Prishtinë, Ferizaj, and with us in Gjilan. People took in strangers. Ismet sheltered around twenty refugees in his house. My cousin Shemsi by this time had built his second house and so gave the first over to a family with five children.

Meanwhile the KLA was no match for the Serbian soldiers and there were terrible setbacks. We heard of the deaths of young men we knew. Commandant Agim Ramadani from near Gjilan was killed on the Albanian border. Another man, Abdullah Tahiri, a political activist and KLA member from

Malisheva, was also killed. A car full of doctors who were helping where they could was shelled and all lost their lives. When the names were read out I learned I knew one of them. He had treated my mother-in-law, Fehime, in her last days.

At this time Albania was making the transition to democracy. Although struggling with poverty, the people there opened their doors to the displaced from Kosova who arrived in ever increasing numbers. In July an arms convoy travelling north from the border was ambushed and seven hundred were killed. We received the news in a deep depression.

I would listen all night to the radio, unable to sleep.

In August we moved into the new house, next door to an old couple, Rama and his wife Nafi, and just four houses along from what had been Sherife's house. Nafi was temporarily bed bound after an operation but the old man was fit and mobile. Ferat had recently remarried and lived there with his new wife. My nephew Adonis, Ferat and Sherife's younger son, had also recently married and lived with them with his wife and their new baby. The older boy, Albert, remained in Prishtinë with our dog, Beta.

Against all that had happened and was likely to happen I was determined to make a home for my family. This was the home I had dreamed of and waited for so many years to enter. I wanted it to be warm and for them to enjoy living here. It felt almost that I could hold no more anxiety and now was compelled to make room for what is good. To my youngest son's delight we acquired another dog.

Part of this home-building was good relations with our neighbours and we made particular friends with Rama and Nafi, whose adult children, two sons and a daughter, had fled seven years before rather than be conscripted into the Bosnian war. Now my boys would do the old couple's shopping and cut their firewood. I still missed Fehime and so was pleased to help Nafi in every way I could, even to the extent of nursing her. She would say after our arrival, 'May God repay your goodness.'

The times were hard but I took refuge in the creation of a 'normal' life. Between us, my husband and I made the house a home and I fed the family as well as I could with, of course, Sherife's words still in my ear. 'Your first responsibility is to those within your doorstep.'

Of course there was no holding the outside world at bay for long. In January another atrocity occurred in Raçak with another slaughter. I was working in the garden one day when Rama came by, his mind and long memory occupied. 'White house, beautiful house,' he said, 'but why are you making a target for them?'

Perhaps we were, but my husband and I were encouraged by events on the international scene. NATO troops had already been assembled in Macedonia. In February the Rambouillet Conference began and, at last, President Rugova was present and therefore recognised. Robin Cook was also present. By March an agreement had been prepared that would safeguard at least our immediate future because Serbia refusing to sign carried with it the certainty of a NATO bombing campaign.

In Kosova we felt that somehow, through the diplomatic mist, Milosevic was staring into the eyes of Robin Cook and that Foreign Secretary Cook would not go home empty handed again. Milosevic would surely not hold out against the inevitable, against the prospect of a bombing campaign that Serbia could not withstand for long. The forces now arrayed against them were infinitely greater than they could muster in defence. The Serbian population, mostly innocent people, would suffer needlessly. No one could believe that he would refuse to sign. Only a madman would hold out.

He refused to sign.

At first we did not really believe the bombing would happen, but when the few European observers in Kosova were evacuated we took it for a sign. On 24 March the first bombs fell. News spread like wild fire.

The planes have taken off from Italy!

The ground shook under our feet.

They've attacked the paramilitaries here in Kosova!

A squadron of bombers passed high overhead.

They've hit Belgrade!

We knew that reprisals would be directed against us and that the numbers of Serbian soldiers in Kosova had already increased. They had automatic rifles, tanks and other sophisticated arms and, without weapons, we had no idea how we might defend ourselves. I went into town to buy first aid equipment and medicines and found that people were buying up flour to make bread, buying food and all kinds of consumables against who knew what length of time.

When I got home Shemsi and Afërdita were waiting to suggest we take refuge in a basement nearby. I asked about my two brothers who lived in that area and about whom we had heard nothing. With its mixed population we swung rapidly from believing that it might be safer for them there to thinking, no, it would be much worse, and back again. With no telephone there was no contact. We worried about Albert, who had been working for the OSCE in Prishtinë. With his employers evacuated, as they must have been, how safe would he be?

Instead of going into the basement we spent that first night with Rama and Nafi, remaining close for protection and comfort. Also with us were another neighbour, Ramadan, his wife and children, boys of an age with my younger two.

There was to be no sleep. In the distance we heard explosions, gun shots, machinery, and we knew that our turn would come. If not this night, it would be the next, or the night after that. Somehow we had to deal with our fear and in this our wise old neighbour Rama was wonderful. He gathered us round him and told us stories of his experiences in the Second World War. He told his stories well and the boys listened with rapt attention, their minds in what was for them the distant past.

When it was time to leave in the morning we said we would come back the next night, but Rama said, 'No, you must find somewhere more secure than this. Did you mention a basement close to here?'

The second night we went down to the centre of town as a family. And yes, in one of the big houses there was a hidden basement, its opening covered with a carpet. There on the cold concrete floor we spent the night with about a hundred others, dreading the moment when the trap door above might be thrown open, listening as the explosions grew closer.

On the third night I took a carpet into the basement for the mothers of younger children to use, but now still more people had arrived. There was not enough space and we were asked to divide our family. I was to remain in the basement with our youngest son while my husband stayed with the older boys upstairs. We went along with this at first but I could not bear it to have the family separated. I took my youngest son by the hand and we went upstairs to find the others. After a short discussion we decided we would return home and let whatever happened happen. Against the possibility of even violent death we would not be parted.

That night we listened to the news on a battery radio, but it was impossible to be sure of anything. The middle and younger boys were exhausted and slept in their clothes on armchairs but our oldest could not sleep any more than we could. By this time he was nineeen years old and very mature and, before we could stop him, he slipped outside to keep watch.

About midnight the village of Llasticë, only six kilometres away on the other side of the hill, was attacked. At night sound travels far, and we heard explosions and gunshots and fighting. Understanding my oldest son was now a young man, I asked my husband to go outside and speak to him and ask him to stay close. Our son simply told him, 'I am not going anywhere', and there was no point in arguing. We all understood that events were working towards some kind of conclusion.

Next day was the Feast of Eid, an important Muslim celebration. Although we had very little to celebrate I decided to make a good meal after so many days of sandwiches. Potato soup and rice – they were the best I could do in the circumstances. We sent some round to Rama and Nafi and so between us, in the hallowing of our traditions and in the giving and receiving of hospitality, asserted our humanity in time of war. With this gesture, and as so often in those days, I felt that Salihe and Sherife were close in spirit.

Outside I joined the boys. It was a bright day and the youngest pointed to a light, a reflection, on the hill opposite that held the underground army base. 'I've never noticed that disc before,' I said. 'It seems to have sprung up overnight.'

Although we could not see it, in the forest a chain saw was

being used to cut timber, and we could hear other, heavier, machinery. We could even hear voices. My oldest son had been watching military trucks and APCs travel back and forth for hours. It was not only the Serbian Army. With the soldiers were paramilitaries and other irregulars. My oldest boy looked at me.

'They're coming for us,' he said.

THE LAST OF THE CLAN

The refurbishment work the City Council has carried out on Kelvingrove Art Gallery and Museum has been completed and a private viewing arranged ahead of the public opening.

Various groups from around the city have been invited and a number of tickets have come to me and, naturally, I have passed them on. We have quite a collection of our own here, of hijabs and headscarves, men and women and children, asylum seekers and volunteers, now scattered through the crowd and exploring the many exhibits and artworks.

There are paintings from Scotland here, especially from the city of Glasgow, from all across the world, sculptures too – an astonishing heritage. In close proximity there are displays on geology, natural history, native peoples and much else. There is a huge menagerie of stuffed animals, an elephant, an elk and all kinds of smaller creatures from foxes to voles. Suspended from the ceiling of one of the chambers, above the giraffe, is a plane, a Spitfire, from the Second World War. If you wish to see it at closer range, eye to eye so to speak, you can do so from the balcony on the first floor.

While you are there, if you look where the pillars meet the roof in huge, supporting arches, you can read the names of great Scots who have contributed to science and the arts through the years, Hutton, Maxwell, Scott, Stevenson and many more. Like the Theatre Royal this building shows what can be achieved when your civilisation is not regularly interrupted by war.

Heather and Charlotte and little David have just left. The couple from Iraq are taking pictures and Nuna is somewhere, but I have lost track. In due course we will meet up. Hijab and other religious clothing does not particularly stand out because

Glasgow now has a substantial population from outside the host community, many of them born here and who have, in fact, joined it. Samira and Zena wander about together, Samira exploring with her usual energetic enthusiasm while Zena looks after a Turkish boy, brother to the little girl I am sitting opposite.

Foot weary I have taken my ease, and a coffee, with one of our volunteers, Helen, and her husband, Tam. Helen, like Janet Andrews, is one of the heroines of the Maryhill Integration Network. The little girl beside her is named Selina and she is the daughter of asylum seekers Sezai and Sultan. The family's case has recently failed and soon they will be sent away. As if this was not bad enough, Sezai has terminal cancer and is undergoing chemotherapy treatment. The stress of the case has been very heavy on Sultan, but not so great as the condition of her husband. Helen looks after the children each weekend and takes them out from time to time, as here today. Eventually she and Tam will have to say goodbye to them, but there will be more like Selina. There are always more.

Suddenly there is a great cacophony from the doors and two pipers enter with a group of dancers in fancy dress. Unusually these are not Scottish pipers. In fact they are from Brittany, in France, and their pipes are higher pitched and more raucous. The ear takes some time to adapt but attention is distracted by the dancers who are dressed in bull-like headgear and tinsel dresses that hang down over their trousers. I think they are women but it isn't easy to tell. They step daintily and pretend to hide behind the exhibits and, it has to be said, Selina is a bit frightened. So much so she cosies into Helen for reassurance and clings to her. The dancers see this and take their attentions across the hall to an older, more confident child.

Later we continue our wander. There is much to do with war in this building, suits of armour, swords and guns. No doubt it has its place but I turn my back on it and, when I do, I come face to face with Thomas Faed's painting *The Last of the Clan*. Located somewhere in the Highlands of Scotland, some time in the nineteenth century, a crowd with an old man at its centre looks from the pier towards a ship that has just left. The ship is out of sight but it takes no great guesswork to understand that the young people have departed and the old man is left behind.

This would be his choice. He would understand that he would be a worry for them on the journey. Besides, they have so much future over there, and so much of his past will always be here. The painting is one hundred and fifty years old but it speaks to me very directly because from personal experience I know what it is to depart from loved ones in the cause of Life. I recognise the truth in this painting.

UNDER ATTACK

In the course of the afternoon Adonis came to visit.

'Tonight we want you to stay with us. We have a basement big enough to hold us all.' Adonis, Meri and their baby boy Andi, together with Adonis's father and stepmother and five of us would make ten in all. We knew the house and felt that, yes, ten people could take refuge there.

My husband was thoughtful, 'Let us weigh things up,' he said.

When Adonis was gone we had a family conference. 'We have Rama and Nafi to think about,' he pointed out. 'They are almost like family now. Nafi is out of bed, but still not fit to travel. Of course Rama will not leave her. How would we feel if anything happened to them?'

But Rama himself had said that we should find a place of greater safety. Since the communal basement was now out of the question, Adonis's offer seemed the best answer. Nowhere would be completely safe, but it could double as both a hiding place and a bomb shelter. In addition it was close by and time was running short. Whatever happened was likely to be very sudden and without warning.

Still my husband was doubtful and it was now, for the first time in their lives, that my oldest son openly disagreed with his father. 'Dad, we have to go,' he said, quite forcefully. 'It is the only choice we can make.'

It would have been an important stage in anyone's growing up but under such circumstances it was particularly poignant. At this time I said nothing.

The boys went round to Sherife's house to see what they could see. They noticed that the basement window showed to the front and guessed it would draw the interest of any ground soldier nearby. They cleaned off the sill and covered the glass as much as possible by piling up rocks. Darkness, they hoped, would do the rest.

I too felt we should follow Adonis but continued to discuss with my husband what might be best. By now it was growing dark and we knew that most massacres happen at night. The boys came back, insisting that we leave right away and really making the decision for us

They returned and my husband visited next door for a quick word with Rama and Nafi to wish them well. Ramadan Salihu and Hajdin Murtezi, other neighbours, were already there. They had decided to stay with the old couple, leaving their own families in their own homes, not far away. Knowing his main responsibility was with us my husband stayed for as long as he could, then, as satisfied as was possible, he walked to Sherife's house.

I was now alone in the home I had dreamed of and that we had built over the years and only entered so recently. In a few short months it had given us many memories and held much love. In important ways the boys had grown up here, but there was nothing to be done. I washed the dishes and put them away, gave the living room a quick tidy and followed.

When we had all arrived Adonis offered to make tea but no one could face it. I looked around but could not see Andi. 'Where is the baby?' I asked Meri. 'Upstairs asleep,' she said. I was suddenly afraid for him. 'Please bring him down,' I asked. 'It's such a distance up those stairs you might not get to him if something happens.'

Meri saw the sense of this and brought the sleeping Andi down. Meanwhile my two oldest boys slipped outside to see what was happening and, in the still of the night, heard the sound of tanks being started among the trees on the hill opposite. From close to the house they saw the long winding curve of the Arkanovci headlights as they drove their APCs down the hillside and into town. There were no street lights so the vehicles lit the sides of the houses as they passed, making mirrors of the windows with their drawn curtains.

At this point the first NATO plane screamed across the sky and the first explosion of the night shook the ground. The APCs stopped and turned off their headlights and the shadow figures of the troops dispersed to either side. The soldiers thought the plane was attacking them, but it had been travelling so quickly that in the time it took for the sound to reach them it was over another Serbian Division. They reformed when it was apparent that the attack had passed them by and once again their headlights lit the sides of the houses as they moved through the streets.

At that point my oldest son said to his brothers, 'You go inside now. I'm feeling cold. I should have brought a pullover. I'm going back to the house to get one.'

The younger boys told me this as they entered and I endured ten blood-freezing minutes until the oldest ran back inside. So much had happened in that time. The line of vehicles had made its way through the streets from the underground base but fired on no one until it reached us. As my son ran back he heard the order given in Serbo-Croat, '*Pali!*' Fire! There had been another enormous explosion and that was all he knew.

We went to the window and looked out. At the bottom of the hill, not far from Shemsi and Afërdita's house, another house was billowing fire and black smoke. It was the house that Kadri Zeka had lived in at the time he was killed. Although Zeka is my family's name, Kadri had not been a relation.

Away back in 1982 he had met with the two Gërvalla brothers, in a village near Stuttgart, with a view to creating a new grouping, the Popular Movement for the Republic of Kosova. To the Yugoslav authorities, particularly the mostly Serbian UDBa, this must have looked like a dangerous combination. As they left their meeting all three men were shot to death in the street. This had occurred seventeen years earlier but memories in the Balkans are long. Now the paramilitaries had gone out of their way to strike that house first and it looked as if it had been specifically targeted. A teenage girl, Zyhrije Pireva, had been killed but at that time my thoughts were with Shemsi and Afërdita.

All ten of us ran downstairs, locking the door behind us. Six adults, three teenage boys and one baby, we were defenceless and helpless beyond the support we could offer each other. From here we could hear everything, shouts, gunshots, grenades. Three or four more explosions went off so close by they felt like earthquakes. Everyone was terrified. I could not get it out of my head, how my oldest son had run in just before the attack began. He had only minutes between being alive or dead. The boys were shivering and said how cold they were. As they wrapped their pullovers around themselves as tightly as they could it was apparent they were in shock. In fact we all were but this was a time we simply had to suffer our way through. Our eyes were on the door as we waited for it to be broken down and the soldiers to appear, or for a grenade to be tossed inside. At one point we could hear their voices close by and their tanks as they ground past, but we could do nothing other than huddle together, staring into the dark and not daring to breathe.

It was to be a centuries-long night and this was just its

beginning. We could not know that the violence had passed us by and was now being visited upon others. Suddenly there was a knocking at the door that quickly turned into an insistent hammering. 'Now we are going to die,' I thought. But then, over the noise of the cannon and guns, we heard a familiar voice.

'It's me! It's me! Remzije, are you there?' It was my cousin Shemsi. We immediately let him in.

'I am so relieved you are here,' he said, running his eye across the group. 'I thought you were dead for sure.'

'Shemsi, what happened?'

'I have bad news. Your house and the house next door have been attacked.' That was Rama and Nafi's house. 'They used their tank cannons on them, and grenades. Some people have been killed. Others are injured, your friend Rama among them. Nafi is all right. We saw the flames from our window and I thought it was you. I ran to see if I could help, but the roof had collapsed and I couldn't open the door. I thought you were inside. My next thought was for Adonis and Meri and the family and here you all are. Thank God.'

They had attacked our house and it was apparent they were taking out specific targets. These choices were not made at random. The paramilitaries had their strategy for these things and had used it since long before Prapashticë. They first identified and killed anyone who might have a leadership role and then took out anyone who might offer resistance. Lastly they murdered and raped the helpless.

I asked myself the question, 'If this is not random, why strike at us?' My husband had been an international sales manager and therefore known abroad. I was the sister of Sherife Rexhepi, an outspoken public figure, and as a radio journalist I was a public figure also. I was daughter of a former senior policeman and carried the name 'Zeka'. Perhaps these things were enough. Rama and Nafi? They lived beside us and they were easy targets, nothing more.

Shemsi would not stay. He returned to help the injured as best he could and then ran for medical help. We remained to protect our children while the minutes went by like months, hours like years.

There was no furniture in the basement, only left over building materials from the house construction. We sat on the floor with our backs to the wall and looked at each other, there was nothing to say, no conversation was possible. We sat looking at each other and listening to the sounds of gunfire and explosions that went on through the night. Shemsi did not return so we had no idea if he was alive or dead. All of us were shivering from a feeling of cold that seemed to come from inside us, not from the floor or surrounding air but from our very bones.

When baby Andi began to cry we were afraid he would alert the soldiers and they would kill us all. We piled our coats and jackets on to him and Meri hushed him back to sleep. Listening to the explosions I could not believe this was happening. Although it made no sense I had a tremendous sense of guilt. What had I done to deserve this? What had I done to bring this on my loved ones? Sleepless and terrified, cold and in silence we passed the night.

In the early hours of dawn with the light beginning to break I went to investigate. The smell of cordite was everywhere. People were moving around in a daze. Already some had loaded such goods as they could onto their backs or into the boots of their cars and were leaving. My husband looked at me and said, 'We have to leave too. There is no choice.'

I approached our house from the rear and immediately understood there was no question of return. My husband went to the garage but the door was jammed. I left him working to get at the car while I went to check on Rama and Nafi. Walking through the mist and smoke someone in passing said to me, 'We are surrounded.'

Rama met me outside his house, his hand swathed in bandages where it had been bruised and burned. 'I had it on the front door handle when the grenade went off, but Remzije that is not the worst.' There was no time for more conversation, only action, but he told me that Nafi was unhurt. Not so the brave neighbours who had remained with them.

The soldiers had known what they were about and planned their assault well, firing their grenades to exactly the same distance from both our houses. Not going for a direct hit, they used flying shrapnel to maximise damage. When the first grenade went off it sprayed the front of our house with metal fragments, pock-marking the walls and shattering the window so that anyone standing behind it would have certainly have been killed.

The second grenade had exploded while Rama and Nafi and the two neighbours were standing in the porch. Ramadan had been killed and the other, Hajdin, severely wounded. He had been struck on the head by shrapnel so that he lost an eye and suffered other injuries, which would later cost him his life. Of Ramadan's body there was no sign other than a mess of blood on the ground and across the wall.

People were now looking in amazement at me as they passed. The ferocity of the attack on our home had been so great that many thought we must surely have been killed.

I went to Ramadan's house to see if there was anything I

could do. There was no sign of his wife, only their two sons crying out, 'Where's my Dad! Where's my Dad!' My own boys came out of the basement then and my middle son was later to say, 'I was not able to cry but my heart was crying instead.' At this time bodies were being carried away covered in blood. He and his older brother went into Rama's garage to take out their car and there they saw parts of Ramadan's body, Ramadan, whom they recognised, limbs, flesh, skin, brain matter spilled. Others lost their lives at the same time, Xhemajl Ymeri, Ramadan Hyseni. Shemsi, thinking of us and of surviving wives and children, had gathered the dead bodies as best he could and taken them into the privacy of the empty garage.

No one should have to see such a sight, and certainly not at such a young age as my boys did.

My husband said to me, 'We can't just leave Rama and Nafi.' We discussed the situation with them and eventually carried Nafi out to the car to take her and Rama into town to a relation of theirs. We would never see them again. Now we had to consider what to do. We did not want to leave Gjilan. If we did we might never get back. We needed time to think and a place of refuge and decided to go to my parents' house. Not only would we be welcome there but we would learn of my brothers and their families and whether they were safe.

The first thing I noticed when we arrived was that the garden gate had been changed and what had once been open and welcoming was now solid and forbidding. This was the house I had been married from in happier times. Then the gate had been open and the house welcoming. Sherife had been alive and well and active and we had been at peace with our neighbours. Looking now at the solid metal door Dad had put up, how could I not remember those days of dressing up and dancing and the promise of happiness?

My brothers and their wives and children were inside. They were waiting for us, and Albert had risked the dangerous journey from Prishtinë to return to the heart of the larger family, my parents, Afiz and Salihe. We were twenty-two people in all. Relieved to see one another, and to learn that no lives had been lost within the family, a casual remark had us all suddenly notice, and agree, that each of us looked older even in this short time.

'And you smell of smoke,' my father said. 'Come inside.'

Naturally everyone wanted to hear everyone else's story. I sat beside Albulena, Ismet's teenage daughter. His son, Ardian, was then nineteen, the same age as my oldest. They had been great friends from birth and almost fell into each others arms. Ismet's two grown-up daughters, Margarita and Arta, were on the other side of town with their own families so we had no news of them. Ahmet's wife, Naza, made tea.

To some extent, in the familiarity of each other's company, we began to relax, but when Naza put the tea down in front of us an astonishing thing happened. For the first time in almost a year I started to bleed. My periods, which had been suppressed by the cancer drugs, now restarted and were to continue frequently and heavily for months. In the midst of all the stress caused by treatments and by the war my body had somehow reasserted itself, but in a way I wished it had not.

We remained in my parents' house for a month, from 28 March to 25 April, living between the basement and the first floor. The ground floor, having been given over to business, was not really suitable. Mostly though, we lived together in a single room for all that time.

Everyone was shattered, stressed in ways that we could not

have even guessed existed. My sisters-in-law, Zana and Ema, hadn't heard from their families in Prizeren and Prishtinë for months. Through those days and nights none of my boys had more than twenty minutes sleep at a time but were wakened by nightmares. Now they had seen what they had seen I found it difficult to look into my children's eyes. It wasn't just that I felt I had failed them; it was a difference in them in that they had seen too much and that some part of them inside had aged beyond their years.

Only my mother went out to the shops to buy what little she could. The Albanian-owned shops had all been broken into and destroyed, their goods stolen. Only those few shops owned by Serbs were open. She would come back with two loafs, sometimes one, and we grew steadily more hungry.

This was the worst month of my life. Every night the electricity was shut off and, sitting in the dark, each one was like a repeat of that first night. NATO planes would fly low over the town to be followed by gunshots, explosions, by the long wait for our turn to arrive. The soldiers and paramilitaries used every NATO strike as an excuse to hit at us.

In the course of the month I rediscovered Ramadan Ibrahimi's book on the massacres at Prapashticë and Keqekollë. It may have been unwise but I found myself dwelling on it in the rare moments of privacy I had. Time and again I would read of such horrors as I knew were being repeated every day, and by the descendants of the same people. I took a fibretip highlighter and marked up the relevant passages, eventually placing it back on the shelf in hope the boys would not find it.

At the end of the first week, my mother returned from the shops empty handed. The shopkeepers were now asking for ID cards just as the paramilitaries were. When her card was handed back to her she had been told, 'Nothing for you, Albanian. Clinton can feed you.'

Albert, Adrian and my oldest took responsibility for keeping watch and not much that happened in the area went unnoticed by them. One night though, I was looking through the window at the high flats opposite when I saw a sniper preparing his position on the roof. It was a commanding vantage point that placed my parents' house in the gunman's sights. If we could see him he could see us. We changed rooms.

After a couple of days my youngest son developed a high temperature and for the following ten days ate nothing, drinking only a very little water. His condition deteriorated rapidly and whether it was the shocks he had suffered, or a virus, or that he had in some way been poisoned, we could not tell, but my husband and I decided we must do something. First we visited the ambulance station but we found only Serbian uniforms hanging at the door and left without asking. Elsewhere, all medical attention was being given to trauma casualties. Again we conferred and this time decided we must go to the hospital at Prishtinë.

My two oldest boys remained with the others, with reassurances of our return, and that all would be well, that we did not feel. I sat in the back of the car with my youngest son's head on my lap and my husband took the wheel to drive north into the teeth of the Serbian ferocity.

As far as was possible he drove off the main roads, frequently over dirt tracks and along paths, to avoid Serbian convoys. It was as if we were travelling through a nightmare land we had never visited before, and not our own countryside that we had known all our lives.

Once again it felt as if we had arrived in a Brothers Grimm tale, or in Grandmother Hamide's storyland of eighty years before. Cars had been crashed and abandoned, houses were on fire. In all the fields dead animals had been left to swell and rot. We passed a group of Serbs barbecuing an animal by the roadside, drinking beer and singing dirty songs about Albanians. NATO planes swept over us and the ground shook with explosions. Most frighteningly, we met with columns of people fleeing the other way.

They came at us with loads on their backs and luggage in their hands, following a tractor towing a trailer loaded with people. All looked at us as if we were mad and many urged us to turn back. We continued though, believing we had no choice, and eventually arrived to find Prishtinë deserted. It was an astonishing other-worldly experience to find the streets we knew so well, that we remembered as bustling, alive and vital, so empty and dead.

Eventually we reached the hospital only to discover it had been turned into an army base. We were met by an orderly and told that no help could be given, that all the patients had been sent home and there was no medical help to be found. At the same time a number of men with big beards were carrying in crates of beer. Of course we remembered that Mihailovic's soldiers had grown such beards during the Second World War to imitate their medieval heroes the Hajduk.

Consumed by desperation and a sense of failure we had no choice but to return through the same hideous landscape. As we drove back we met the same bedraggled column we had met on our way out, wearier now. Having almost reached Gjilan, they had been stopped and turned back. This was a demoralising tactic of the Serbs that was not new. We later learned that, in the village of Perlepnica, the Imam had been sent up onto the minaret of his Mosque to call out that all Albanians were to leave within the following twelve hours. Their miserable column had been forced to walk itself into exhaustion before it was turned back to find Perlepnica in flames. And then it was turned again.

Our son was no better and perhaps even worse for making the journey. We got back safely though, and then – miracle! A local nurse located some antibiotics and administered them by injection over a period of days. Afraid it might be a virus, and so contagious, he and I retreated to the top floor of the house and there I nursed him back to something like health.

My brother Ahmet, the engineer, located a small electricity generator and set it up in the house. This allowed us to power the radio and television and suddenly we were much better informed. We discovered that some of our television journalists had escaped to Albania and were broadcasting from there. In addition Radio 21, American Radio and Free Europe were more active than ever.

All night we sat listening to the news, none of it good. One hundred were killed here, one hundred and fifty there, mostly men. Different groups were being targeted, including everyone associated with the OSCE. On two occasions already the police had forced entry to the house in search of my brothers, and if they had found them we might all have been killed. They remained a step ahead.

On 24 April we received information that the paramilitaries would be coming for them next day. We were cold, hungry and growing weaker. In addition my frequent heavy periods had left me anaemic. Everybody understood we were coming close to the end and that something had to be done.

We sent the children, all of them, upstairs and then were free to discuss our situation. Our position was impossible but no course of action was safe or even acceptable. Flight south to Macedonia, we agreed, would be suicidal, but so would remaining in Gjilan. Feelings ran high as we argued it out, and we were as determined not to leave our parents as they were that we should.

'Think of your children,' my mother said. 'You must take them away to Macedonia. No one knows what will happen there but at least they will be out of present danger.'

'And you, what about the two of you?'

'We will stay,' said Dad. 'No point in leaving Kosova. We have lived here too long not to be buried here now.' Of course we understood they were afraid of being a burden to us, of slowing the journey and endangering us. The idea of leaving them was sickening.

'Who will look after you?'

'We have good neighbours, but they are quite rightly afraid that the search for OSCE people will endanger them. It is best for them also that you leave. They send their promise to stay with us for as long as possible.'

'You've been speaking with them then.'

'Look,' said Dad. 'You may give yourselves only one chance in a hundred by leaving, but stay here and you will have none.'

We went round the group. No one was prepared to leave but Agim was most committed to staying.

'We cannot give up without a fight,' he said.

'A fight,' said my father, 'and what will you fight with? You have no weapons.' He went into another room and returned with his old police helmet. 'Look,' he said. 'This is all we have.

Take that upstairs to the children. Wrap it round them and protect them that way.'

'It is not right that we leave without one of us giving his blood for Kosova,' Agim said.

Still a strong man, broad, powerful in the shoulder, my father stretched to his full height to reply. 'Kosova has had enough of blood! Do you want no one with the name of Zeka to remain alive?'

There was a silence that stretched far into the night until my mother broke it with her terrible pledge that I will remember all my life. She touched her breasts with both hands and drew them forward as if she was making an offering. 'By the milk I gave you when I gave you birth,' she said, 'I beg you to leave.'

The decision was made. It was the hardest decision of all our lives.

Before first light the twenty of us who were leaving piled into three cars and set out. There was hardly room to breathe and we could only hope we would not be stopped on the way, but we were moving. Once again we had hope. The neighbours, strong people and good, came out to stand with our parents as my husband gunned the engine and I looked from the car window. That is my strong memory of them, together at the door of our childhood home, the home of so many memories and so much happiness.

Both stood straight and as tall as they could, my father's arm resting across my mother's shoulder. She, Salihe, was dry eyed, allowing no room for a change of mind or future regret. My father though, Afiz Zeka, really Doda, born of the mountainous border country, who had married our mother there, Sherife's and mine, fought across it to defend their home and future, who had come down onto the plains when he judged it wise and even changed his name, who had made a career and broken it rather than betray his people, who had been strong for us and made us strong, protected and defended us and guided us all our lives, he wept there; he broke his heart.

The information we had received proved to be correct. The police arrived the next day but found the place empty. They wrecked it in their top to bottom search but found no one and nothing. My parents were hiding in a neighbour's basement and we had been on the road for hours.

JUST AN OLD BOOK

Once again I sit behind my desk in the tiny office above the Drop-In.

The main doors are closed so the Bible Study class can gather round a table and discuss, today, Ecclesiastes. As I passed them Lydia was reading, 'There is a time for everything, and a season for every activity under heaven: a time to be born and a time to die, a time to plant and a time to uproot.'

Although not from a Christian background, my parents would have understood this because the instinct for continuance lives in the bone's marrow and will not be gainsaid even by the instinct for survival. I have long since recognised the necessity of separating the head's workings from those of the heart but the power of affection at times is simply too strong. The tears in my eyes do no one any good.

The helmet Dad used in his argument was the helmet he used as a policeman and he believed its presence, if found, could compromise our safety. When we, the younger generation who were also the generation with responsibility for children, finally accepted that our parents would have their way my father took it upstairs and used a pair of pliers, the kind used for stripping electrical flex, to cut it into tiny pieces. It took him hours to complete the job and by the end his wrists were aching, but if the Serbian forces had found it they would have killed everyone who remained in the house.

When he was done he put the pieces in a plastic bag and buried them in the garden and there they remained for many months. None of the searches were so thorough as to dig up the garden. They were not the only betraying object to be buried there.

From the desk drawer here in my office I take my copy of Ramadan Ibrahimi's book on the massacres of 1921 and examine the cover, the copyright page and the notes at the end. When we were gone my mother placed it also in a plastic bag and buried it in another spot. I flick through the pages, examining it thoroughly and studying the sentences I highlighted and referred to through that long, terrible month in Gjilan.

The world knows now that my fears of that time came to pass and the atrocities were repeated, as they had been repeated over and again through the first part of the twentieth century, back in time through the centuries, to the Battle of Kosova in 1389, usually with the complicity of some Great Power seeking influence and gain. They have been repeated even as an opera is repeated, like *Carmen*, always with the same shocking events leading to the same tragic ends.

After KFOR arrived Mum still did not know where we were or if we were alive. In that time she dug the book up and slept with it under her pillow. She said it made a sort of connection with me and, through me, with the rest of the family. When eventually we made contact she sent it to me, this very copy.

Since those desperate days of our flight we have all been back to Kosova. Reconnections have been made and, to our delight, our youngest son has not only met but married a most beautiful girl. Although he is now a fully fledged British citizen the Home Office still takes a cautious view of 'immigrants through marriage'. As in all things we work steadily towards her arrival and soon her application for a visa will be considered. We write to the British Embassy in Macedonia, as do my son's many friends, and we wait in hope. Meantime we maintain such connections as we can, some material, some less so.

I hold the book more reverently now than ever before. I run my fingers gently across the cover and down the spine.

BORDER CROSSING

The streets of Gjilan were deserted when we left.

Only the trucks parked by the police station and APCs parked by the hospital where ambulances should be indicated any kind of life at all. Getting out of town without being stopped was our first worry.

The early hour and luck saw us through. Now we had thirty kilometres before us before we got to Ferizaj, another twenty to Kaçanik, from there another fifteen to Blacë and the border crossing and Macedonia. It was a journey we had made many times before, when Sherife was ill, when I was, and in better times for all kinds of mundane reasons such as shopping. It was no great distance, but we made the journey unsure that we would even survive, far less arrive safely. It was made all the longer by having to go round the main towns using side roads.

It was springtime in Kosova and the greening hills to either side looked almost as if they were etched onto the sky so clear was the light. Driving through the broad Morava Valley in those anxious hours we could have no thoughts for the landscape we loved and had known since childhood. There was no movement on the road other than our own but, as when we had driven to Prishtinë and the hospital, there were signs of the disaster everywhere. Villages lay in ruins, animals dead in the fields. No one so much as looked from a window and there was no movement in the valley at all.

Again and again we came across the blackened hulks of burned-out cars and after the first few I did not allow myself to look because of the bodies inside. Here and there houses were on fire. Some were already burned down to charred skeletons.

Our great fear was that we would be stopped, that the men

would be separated from the women, that the men would be killed and the women raped. Whenever possible our drivers chose back roads in hope of greater safety, my husband always steady with his eyes on the road ahead until, between Ferizaj and Kaçanik, we came to a road block and were forced to halt. The soldiers came round with their guns at the ready.

'Are you armed?' they demanded. Of course we had neither guns nor any other weapon. 'Step out! If we find so much as a bullet you will pay for your lie.'

We got out of the cars.

'Let's see your ID,' they demanded. We had our cards that identified us as Albanians, not that the soldiers would have been in any doubt that we were just that and that we were fleeing to the border. Later we discovered that one and a half million people had been made homeless, many of them hiding in the hills. Others had been streaming in this direction ever since. Many, as we had seen, had been murdered on the way.

They searched the cars but did not find their bullet.

'What money do you have?' they demanded. This had been expected, although they might as easily have searched our dead bodies. Before setting out I had removed all my jewellery, making a point of removing even the most stubborn ring because we knew they were as capable of cutting off a living finger as a dead one in their thieving. Our men handed over such cash as they had and, after they tore up our ID, we were sent onwards.

In the car I looked at the boys and feared they would never recover.

Five or six kilometres before the border we were stopped again. This time we were told to get out of the cars and continue on foot.

At this location there is a break in the hills, a pass that has been travelled since human beings first arrived in the Balkans. Through it runs the River Lepenc on its way to become the Vardar, and the disused railway and the main road from Prishtinë. There is a concrete block house at the crossing point and fences, but these had never been true barriers before. Now, as we supported each other along the road, we looked first in wonder, then in horror at what lay ahead of us.

A huge crowd of people was waiting on the Kosovan side with streams of newcomers making their way towards it from all directions, wherever there was a track of any kind. In tattered columns or small groups they walked the roads as we did, or held to old hillside paths or the disused railway line. Some were being tractor-hauled on trailers. Some, very few, were in cars. By far the greatest number were on foot like us. Old women in headscarves walked hand in hand with old men in their Albanian bonnets. Some younger women were pregnant, many were ill. Those who had not been robbed of everything carried some kind of burden on their backs. One pair carried a stuffed holdall between them.

When we eventually joined the great mass of people we learned that some had been waiting for as long as four days. There were no toilets, no fires or cooking facilities, no accommodation or cover of any kind. In the course of their waiting some of the pregnant women gave birth to their babies without medical aid. Strong gusting winds blew rain across the valley and people were soaked to the skin. Between storms they would dry where they stood.

It was raining when we arrived. Under the overhang of the block house roof there might have been room for one hundred or so people to take shelter, but the Serbian guards would not let anyone near. On the other side their Macedonian equivalents were out of sight, but the hillsides stretched on unchanging as they always had. We gathered in our family group that had somehow, against expectation, survived together and began our wait.

We were among the lucky ones in that the next batch was to be allowed through not long after our arrival. Twenty-four hours later the crowd was called to line up on the road. There were two corridors through the block house but we were forced into a single line. This did not produce an efficient system of transfer but people were too exhausted and frightened to argue.

Border guards walked up and down the line carrying guns and long plastic batons, the kind with an additional handle at the side so they can be used in different ways, two-handed or as prods.

The road was a single carriageway with a broken white line down the middle. This they used as a device to keep us in order, insisting that we remain on the right side of the line although we were several bodies deep as pressure from the rear forced us to take up the full width. Anyone who put so much as a foot on the line they struck on the leg with their batons. I know this too well because I was one of them, but this was not the worst thing to happen.

I kept my youngest son close to me and my hands on him as much as possible because he was exhausted and ill as well as starving and cold. As a guard walked past my boy blacked out and collapsed, half unconscious, across the line. The guard already had his baton to hand and immediately began to hit my son where he lay, across the shoulders, across the body, shouting at him to get back in line.

Without thinking I threw myself on top of him but the guard would not stop hitting. Our desperate situation, and I suppose adrenaline, meant I hardly felt the blows as I used my knees and elbows to drag us both back across the line. It happened very quickly and our men wisely did nothing. By this time their physical strength together could not have matched the guard so weakened were we. By confronting him, certainly by laying hands on him, they would have brought on all our deaths.

We waited in line for two hours before we finally edged through the corridor and set foot in Macedonia. By no means safe at least now we would not be shot. With my first step I turned and looked back at the hills of Kosova with powerfully mixed feelings of loss and relief. Against all odds we had completed our journey and survived, but my parents were still in Gjilan and whether they were alive or dead I could not know.

Dad had said one chance in a hundred. Even with that in mind we had not anticipated what we had witnessed, the devastated villages, the road block, burned-out cars, the suffering crowd and the border guards. Only now did my body ache where the baton had struck. I thought about my parents and how we could get word back that we had survived. Of course it was impossible. I remembered Hamide's mother, my great-grandmother, who fled and never returned, how she had never seen her daughter again. Now I feared history was repeating itself and, like her, I could not say goodbye in my heart.

Yet we had survived, my husband and I had survived. The boys were safe and, in time, their bodies would recover. I prayed that their minds and souls would also recover.

Explosions were still happening on the Kosova side of the border, gunshots, shouting. People continued to crowd through the block house while the aid agencies closed in on us. There was a great confusion in which earlier refugees came searching for loved ones. Names were called out, the names of places, the names of families. Ismet looked anxiously for his two adult daughters, Margarita and Arta, but they were not to be seen. Buses took us into the town of Blacë, no great distance, to a tented village where we would spend the rest of the night. But the tents were too crowded. No one could lie down far less sleep, and in the end we went out and sheltered under the flyleaf to watch the rain teeming down. As explosions continued across the border, I understood beyond doubt that my heart and mind were still there and always would be.

The morning of the 26th was bright and sunny and so offered some measure of relief. The Red Cross arrived and told us we would be taken to the camps, Stankovec One and Stankovec Two. Buses were provided and, as we climbed into them, we could see over the heads of the crowd the refugees who were still streaming through in their thousands. In the confusion my husband was separated from the boys and me when we were told to transfer from one bus to the other, from Stankovec One to Two. We were also separated from Adonis, Meri and Andi at this point and did not see them again. There were special provisions there for the children but all was confusion until suddenly, the Macedonian police were waving their arms in front of the bus and we were moving.

We travelled for forty or fifty minutes until we came to a bare and treeless hill with an even greater tented village, surrounded by a high fence and barbed wire. Men in uniforms were on patrol and, at first, this was disturbing. Men in uniforms had been intimidating us for so long that we had become conditioned and fearful and, in fact, it would take many months to even begin to get over it. I braced myself, wondering how strong I would have to be, and for how long, and then saw that some of the French soldiers were playing football with the children. I cannot describe the feeling of relief at seeing soldiers behaving in this way. This simple, normal piece of fun was in stark contrast to the terror we had left behind where the murder of children had become normal.

To his astonishment Ismet met some of his students who knew Margarita and Arta. 'They've been here for days,' they told him. 'You almost missed them. They're being evacuated now – right now!'

They had walked together to the border, Arta with her baby daughter and Margarita pregnant, and it was a miracle they had survived. Ismet dashed across the camp and was just in time to wave to them as they left. He had not managed so much as a word of reassurance and love but had at least seen that they were alive and they had seen him.

The Red Cross and other international charity organisations were efficiently equipped with names and lists and order was slowly established within the confusion. We were reunited with my husband and taken to a makeshift shelter that could hardly be described even as a tent. Lengths of canvas material were propped up on strips of wooden plank. Plastic groundsheets covered the grass and of this we had to make some kind of home for we did not know how long.

The sound of explosions was more distant now, but I still found it impossible to escape the oppression of war. Although thousands of people were walking about, and French soldiers were everywhere, I did not have a feeling of real security. There was no way of escaping worry about those left behind, my parents of course, but also the neighbours who had helped, and my husband's sisters. More, there could be no sense of settlement while shattered, weeping people kept coming in, and they did so all the time.

Our men made themselves useful by erecting more shelters on the outskirts of the camp and I could not help but notice how close they had become and how protective. All of them were much weakened by the experiences of many months but they seemed to take strength from this activity. The camp by now was like a small city. So big was it that my Aunt Sofie was on the other side and we never met or so much as knew she was alive. Ema, Agim's wife, met her older brother, who had been in the camps for more than two months, but at that time neither of them knew the circumstances of the rest of their family. None of us could guess what the future held but to be still breathing was enough. We contributed what we could by way of effort and caring and were grateful to be alive.

We were given cold tinned food by the Red Cross and by the French soldiers as well as blankets and sleeping bags. Toilets were rudimentary, wooden poles with blankets stretched between and pits dug in behind. Even now I shudder when I think of them. There were no washing facilities, no running water at all other than what fell from the sky. I had never been so dirty in my life. But now, of course, we were unaware even of the smell because we had been living with it for so long and were so pressed by matters of life and death. Our most overpowering emotions at the time were relief and gratitude.

All of us, everyone in the camps, were survivors and all had stories to tell. I told mine and listened to other women as they spoke of the familiar patterns of invasion, separation of men and women and what followed. As so often through the decades, through the centuries, the overpowering, consistent theme was one of wanton cruelty. We heard of the village where over a hundred men were shot in front of their women's eyes.

Afterwards they, the women, were told to 'go to Albania where you belong', but two old women were disabled and could not walk with the others. The Arkanovci piled timber around their wheelchairs and burned them to death.

In another village they burst in on people while they ate. 'What's this?' they said, looking at the bean stew being prepared. 'Don't you normally have meat with this?' They took a fourteen-year-old boy, lopped off his fingers and threw them in the pot. 'Eat that now,' they said. The boy later died of blood loss and shock.

We kept our eyes open for newcomers from Gjilan and after ten or twelve days we discovered a neighbour, falling on her for news even as people had fallen on us when we arrived. The latest was that my parents were alive! This was when we learned of the police search on the day after our leaving. We also learned that Mum and Dad had gone from one neighbour's basement to another on successive nights to share the risk and to confuse the police if that was possible.

Only three days earlier my mother had been seen in a bread queue on the far side of Gjilan from her home. She had been hungry but alive and that was the end of the news. There was nothing to be understood from this about my father's fate but we knew that men simply could not appear out of doors or they would be killed.

These few words represented only a small hope but I placed it in my heart and held it there.

One day I did my usual self-examination and discovered a small lump on my remaining, left, breast. I decided to say nothing to my husband, and certainly not to the boys or my brothers, because there was no point in piling another anxiety onto them. Instead I went to the hospital tent with an interpreter and saw a French doctor there. Suspected cancer was out of their normal routine, which, of course, was focused on trauma and shock. On first examination she could not discover anything and even called other doctors across. They all tried but found nothing. Perhaps under these conditions and with so much weight loss I was particularly sensitive. At any rate I was very certain. I took the first doctor's finger in my hand and guided it to the spot and pressed it in. 'Ah, yes,' she said. 'There is something there. It's a rudimentary diagnosis but ...'

She put our name down for immediate evacuation on medical grounds and at this point it became apparent that the family was breaking up. This was another great pain but there was no question of opposing the process. The only alternative for us was to accept, to go where fate took us, and promise to reconnect when we could.

Agim and Ahmet left for Austria and safety on 6 May.

By now developments were happening again on the political scene. The wider international public had become aware of our plight and their sympathy was aroused. The artist Richard Geary visited the camps and, after him, the British Prime Minister, Tony Blair. 'Thank God,' I thought, 'the world can see what is going on.'

Immediately after this, Great Britain decided to help with the evacuation. That Saturday at dusk a van went through the camps and an announcement was made by megaphone. 'Tonight there will be a list posted of families who will be sent to the United Kingdom.'

We were visiting another family in Stankovec Two when the boys were told by one of their friends that our name was on the list. Despite all that was happening I could not bear the thought of leaving. The call of my homeland and the fate of my loved ones were very strong in my system, but sometimes you have to fight your emotions and do what is best rather than what you want. Sherife's words sounded in my head again. 'You have to look after those within your own doorstep.' We had no doorstep any more but there could be no doubt about the choice.

On the Monday we were taken by bus to Skopje Airport and there we boarded a Bulgarian plane operated by Macedonians. It was a journey of the wounded and the sick. Men were carried aboard on stretchers, women hobbled up the ramp on crutches. Five of us had been diagnosed with cancer. I was one of them and another was a young boy who had leukaemia.

Two planes took off that day. We were in the second and only now did we realise how awful our condition must appear to those who were helping us. The air crew all wore surgical gloves and white surgical masks to protect them from the danger of infection. Only when we were on board did we learn exactly where we were going: to Glasgow in Scotland.

A few years later one of my sons would write that he did not even know if Scotland was an English-speaking country – not that any of us spoke any English. My husband's interest in sport, which he had handed on to his sons, meant we had heard of the two famous football teams, Rangers and Celtic. We also knew of kilts and bagpipes because those are the two great symbols of Scotland abroad. We could relate to them because Albanians also have kilts and bagpipes.

These were the few sketchy indications we had of our destination when the engines fired up and propelled us along the runway and into the sky.

BEGINNING AGAIN

Today I am working from home; my husband and the boys are out so I have the place to myself.

The great, good news is that my daughter-in-law's visa has been granted and, since she arrived, all our lives have changed for the better. Everyone is so much happier but especially, of course, my son. The visa will last for two years and then she will apply for permanent residency.

Not everything goes so well. The Oasis Women's Group is no more secure now than when we first heard that funding was being withdrawn. I keep knocking on doors and filling in applications. This is why I work from home today. The computer in my office has no access to the internet. Therefore Community Planning Partnership's application form has to be completed and emailed from here.

Soon Sharon will arrive with numerous files under her arm and we will complete the form together and send it back with our fingers crossed. We are well aware there is only so much money to go round and that officials have to choose between many worthwhile projects. There is an element of competition I would rather was not there because all of us at the Maryhill Integration Network only wish those other projects well.

So we will fill in the form as well as we are able and then turn to another, this time for the Glasgow Anti-Racist Alliance. If successful this will help us continue with many other projects besides the Oasis Women's Group, but especially in celebrating Black History Month.

There is no end to the filling in of forms, but there is no end to any aspect of what we do. Sharon, I know, puts in more hours than she is paid for or that we ask of her. Recently she arranged acupuncture for Sezai, little Selina's father, in hope of controlling the pain of his cancer. Earlier, when a homeless asylum seeker broke down under the stress of his position she helped him find new accommodation.

In these things Sharon is tireless, and tonight we will return to the Drop-In. There are people there waiting for us, people who depend on us. We do not want to let them down, and there are always more of them. New cases go before the Home Office every day. A huge proportion of our time is spent in providing assistance and advice to asylum seekers but we have to secure funding. We are continually beginning again.

MAKING A NEW LIFE

The dispossessed and displaced are first of all exhausted, then life returns.

On the plane our thoughts had ranged back to Gjilan and forward into an unpredictable future. The boys were thin and ill and suffered from nightmares. My husband had lost at least twenty kilograms and I was no better, but now at last we saw light ahead.

An interpreter had been sent from the UK to help and he told us about medical help and other aid that would be waiting for us at Glasgow Airport. This seemed beyond belief but, when we landed, more than one hundred people were waiting. Twenty of them were young Albanian interpreters who had left in earlier years rather than be conscripted to fight in Bosnia and Croatia. Identified by the orange tops they wore, all had tears in their eyes at what they saw.

Inside we were met by officials from the Home Office, Social Services, Education and charities such as the Red Cross. All around were hygiene packages containing soap, toothpaste, clean underwear, unimaginable luxuries in the circumstances.

Right then and there we were given dinner and I asked myself if this was a dream I would wake from back in Hell. For many months we had not seen a smile or heard a welcome, now they were all around. We were given introductions to the individuals who were assigned to help us and our photographs were taken for future identification. Certificates that declared our right to remain for one year were placed in our hands.

We were led out to another bus and driven through Glasgow to our new homes, although some were taken directly to hospital. For over a year we had been without much electricity, certainly not enough to illuminate Gjilan. Night-time Glasgow was brilliant with street lights and lights from windows and on high buildings and we realised that civilised life had become a half forgotten memory – but not wholly forgotten.

At Red Road, lists had been posted matching family names to flat numbers. When we entered ours my eye fell on the cut flowers that had been placed there by some other woman acting, not out of necessity or duty, but from the goodness of her heart.

We entered our new home on the twenty-sixth floor of the Red Road flats in a bewildered condition. In a matter of a few hours we had been transported from the crowded Stankovec Two to a private place of our own. It was furnished, warm, dry, and there were fresh cut flowers in the living room, bananas and chocolate in the kitchen. My boys had not eaten chocolate for over a year. Best of all though, we were safe. The feeling of being at war was left behind and we were free. Clean at last, well fed, safe, we slept for hours.

For days I had been coming to realise the extent of our good fortune. For all we had witnessed, and for all the starvation and sacrifice, terror and near death events, our family had escaped without loss of life. Many other families had been wiped out completely. Women no different than me had seen their loved ones tortured, raped and murdered before their eyes. In terms of personal injury we had not suffered so much as a broken fingernail.

What we could not appreciate at that time was the great difference between the way we Kosovars were treated and that of others in flight. We had been immediately recognised as refugees, rather than asylum seekers and so had the right to participate fully in society where they do not. This does not dilute my appreciation and gratitude for the generosity and acceptance my family has received, but it does recognise a difference I was soon to witness at close hand and now work with every day.

My thoughts now turned to establishing the family in this new country, and to my own health. At that time we had no intention of remaining for the rest of our lives. After some indefinite period of time Kosova would be rebuilt, but there was no telling how long our stay would be.

In these things, as in all things, we were helped by the Kosovan Programme Team on Glasgow Refugee Council and the team of interpreters who were never far away. Over the next two days representatives of different agencies came by with forms for us to complete. We discussed the flat with them, financial and social arrangements and our whole situation. The boys were to be taken into Hillhead School, some distance away, where the services of the interpreters would be vital to their settling in and to their progress.

My health condition was at a stage where tests were required, rather than urgent surgical intervention or therapy. At Stobhill Hospital the doctors were already in possession of the diagnosis made in Stankovec Two. I was examined with the use of a mammogram and a sample was taken for biopsy, but this was just the start. I had to wait a month for the results and when they arrived I was put on the list for surgery. In that time of waiting I realised that I did not want, could not allow myself, to sit thinking about the past. Over the years that preceded the catastrophe we had developed a system of mutual aid in Kosova that included education, health and sanitation. What it amounted to was a culture of volunteering and, because of this, I knew what my new direction must be.

I still had not heard from my parents and there was no telephone connection to Kosova. Using the Library Internet Service I visited the United Nations web site and learned figures that shocked even me. Serbian forces had killed eleven thousand people in Kosova, 90% of them women, children and old people. Four thousand more had disappeared and another two thousand had been imprisoned. Some four hundred and forty-three thousand refugees had fled to Albania, two hundred and forty-seven thousand to Macedonia and almost seventy thousand to Montenegro. An astonishing twenty-one thousand had found their way to Bosnia. Others were dispersed across Europe to a total of eight hundred and sixty thousand lost souls.

Again using the Library Internet Service I made contact with journalists in Albania. Radio 21 had moved from abroad closer to home and soon I was sending short reports to them, and to Albanian television, about the wonderful reception we had received in Glasgow. I asked the television people to please put a sub-text across the bottom of the screen saying 'Remzije Sherifi is safe in Glasgow. Can the family please get in touch?'

One by one the dispersed family came through by email. All three of my brothers were in Austria, although in different locations. Aunt Sofie was in Sweden. Some cousins were in Switzerland, another was in Canada. Adonis, Meri and Andi were in Turkey. Albert was also in Sweden. Then it happened. A phone call from the United Nations in Prishtinë – and it was my mother's voice! She had heard of my plea and moved heaven and earth to get to the only telephone possible and, yes, she and Dad were both well. We did not have long to speak but had time to reassure each other and talk about the boys.

At this time I had no English, but realised I would have to set about learning the language as quickly as possible. In this the interpreters and case workers who had been assigned to me, Frida and Flutra, were very important. In fact, we became great friends very quickly.

When the social worker, Margaret Ferguson, visited I asked if I could do some kind of voluntary work, perhaps with Albanian children. Some were at school now and beginning to learn English. Their minds had not been properly engaged with education for years because, although we had done our best with the parallel education system, moving from house to house and constantly changing teachers has built-in limitations.

Together with Clare O'Hara, drama specialist, we organised a cross-cultural *ceilidh*, and I learned not only a new word but of the existence of another language, Gaelic, that gave it to English. The performance was called *Castle and Kelpie* and we presented it as part of a summer programme designed to share Albanian culture with that of the surrounding community. The Scottish *Kelpie* legend is that of the water horse; the *Castle* is the castle that three Albanian brothers worked on each day in Kosova, but which was broken down by others at night so that no progress was ever made. Clare and I worked through Frida, and Clare passed on the words to the children.

My operation was scheduled for 8 September, which by coincidence is the birthday of both of Sherife's sons. Thinking of her again I could not help but notice a difference in myself. This time I did not have the anxiety, I mean the cancer related anxiety, I had endured in Kosova when the illness was first diagnosed. This time I felt I could face and accept whatever fate and medical science might present.

Once again my husband was a tower of strength. He had prepared the boys as best he could but it was apparent that their fears were greater than mine. After all they had been through it was not surprising. I was comfortable, myself, with living or dying, but the last thing they needed now was to lose their mother. Seeing this clearly, and knowing the suffering Albert and Adonis had gone through when Sherife died, I resolved to do all I could to remain alive for them.

I sometimes say, 'I live for my boys'. Not everyone understands how literally true this is. They are the light of my life.

My husband came with me to hospital on the day of the operation. So did Frida, who even wanted to come into theatre with me while the lymph glands were removed. When they were tested the growths proved to be benign and for the time being I was safe, but the lesson about the importance of staying alive for those who love me and need me remained.

My consultant, Mr Hansell, had something to say beyond the immediate treatment of my condition. He was concerned about a return to Kosova where the health infrastructure was substantially broken down. 'The cancer could return any time,' he said. 'Speedy diagnosis and treatment are so important I feel you should think very hard about remaining permanently. If you do go back and the cancer returns you might die for lack of treatment.'

Three months later, after a regular check-up, a suspicion formed that the cancer might have moved into my bones. The particular area of suspicion was my ribs and I was asked if I had suffered a childhood injury in that area. Back in our flat at Red Road we had a family discussion and decided that we should remain if it was possible. Of course my parents were still at the forefront of my mind and I wondered if I would ever see them again. In fact the suspicion proved to be wrong, but the anxiety continued. The doctors obviously felt the cancer could return at any time and in places other than my breast.

Elated by this reprieve I sent an article off to a women's magazine that was now being republished in Kosova. In it I was able to report not only on how well we were being treated but that Albanian culture was being preserved and cultivated among our young people. By now the rest of the family were making their ways back. I was reconciled to never being able to return permanently but I felt it as a pain in my heart. I assured the readers that those of us who stayed had good reasons. Of the two hundred and ninety-six who had arrived together all had needed medical treatment and twenty-seven cases had been so urgent their survival had depended on it.

Happy to be free and safe and with the opportunity of work, I was beginning to feel my life was complete again. In a different way, I was becoming more complete as a human being. Amazingly, new fields were opening for me in education and with refugees. Even my small offerings of journalism had been accepted. Still too piecemeal and vague to be seen for what they were, new directions and purposes were forming.

About the time we arrived in Glasgow an organisation named Glasgow Caring City was formed by Protestants, Catholics and Muslims working together to help support Albanian refugees. Of course I became involved, finding myself giving emotional and practical aid to people who were too afraid, or physically incapable of leaving their homes. I also helped in Scottish Refugee Council projects. Voluntary work proved to be a route for me not only into activity and usefulness but into friendships and unofficial support systems. In my work now I always encourage asylum seekers along this route and ease their way as best I can. At the very least it puts their feet on the ladder.

Glasgow Caring City does much good work in collecting clothes that are being discarded by better-off people and distributing them among the asylum seekers and refugees. In addition they took supplies back to Kosova to help relieve the many casualties. Although Glasgow Caring City was founded especially to assist us it still exists and assists in crisis locations all over the world.

One day, with others, I was taken by minibus to their warehouse to sort through the clothes that had been donated and see if anything was of use to my family. On that occasion I did not take anything but was able to help a number of other women. Among them was one young woman who had lost her twin sister in the war, another young woman who was recovering from throat cancer and a third who was obliged to use crutches.

For some reason this took the eye of Margaret Galbraith, the wife of Neil Galbraith, a Church of Scotland minister who was deeply involved with the charity. She must have heard me mention that 23 June is our wedding anniversary and noted that it was coming up. On that day someone phoned to say that we would have visitors and Margaret turned up with a bouquet of flowers. Another friend was made.

Neil made regular visits to Kosova and, because I was now in touch with Radio 21, between us we were able to arrange a broadcast link and do a live programme. Eugen Saraçini, director of the station, took the microphone in Prishtinë, with Neil and others as his guests, and I did the same in Glasgow. We conducted interviews, conversations, played music, and I felt as if I was a working journalist again.

Early in 2000 we learned that the UK's Humanitarian Aid

Programme would take one member of each refugee family back for a week's stay. We had a long discussion on which of us should go and, because of my health and my parents' age, decided it should be me on this first occasion. In February I returned. The reunions were deeply emotional and this time it was Mum who cried.

Returning from Glasgow I looked at Kosova with a new eye. Much that I loved was gone. One hundred and twenty thousand houses had been destroyed. To my great sorrow, I learned that five hundred of our schools were in ruins, along with many mosques. For the first time in our long history Albanians had turned in anger on some Serbian churches. These were not the long established monasteries of the Serbian Orthodox Church but smaller buildings established by the Milosevic regime to enhance its territorial claims. During the war they had been used as military bases.

I also learned that many Serbian people had fled to the north in fear of reprisals. Many will have been complicit in the persecution of the Albanian people, others innocent but still afraid. Sixteen thousand Croatian and Bosnian Serbs who had been settled among us during the wars of the preceding decade also left. City dwellers who had taken no part in the persecutions but could not face the returning Albanians left to live in the Serbian villages of Kosova.

The economy had broken down even before the violence worsened so rapidly. Employment was down to about 20% and wages among those few who had work were at minimal levels. Even now tremendous effort must still be made to bring my country up to normal European standards, so much so it will continue far beyond my lifetime. Enormous investment is required and success will require peace over such a duration as we have never known.

Ahmet took me up to our house, the one we had built through such difficult and changing times and eventually had to flee from. 'You'd best be prepared for a shock,' he said.

'Shocks?' I replied. 'These days they're my way of life.'

He had done whatever repairs on the house were possible, cleaning out the mess and replacing the windows. In place of our lovely red roof he had tied sheets of corrugated iron. Kosova, of course, was now a country of internal displacement. Whole families would have no place to stay until the building programme caught up with them. A family of thirteen were living there with our full knowledge and permission, only the latest. I was pleased that our home was being used to help people in need. We could make no long term plans. Let happen whatever good might come of it.

Everyone hungered for news from everyone else and the week passed in a welter of stories. In all our family only one had lost his life. In this way we were lucky although the sorrow and grief was no less for him than it would have been for any loved one who was lost in an accident or to illness. The great numbers and the size of the tragedy did nothing to lessen the effect of each death.

Cousin Gani was the son of Uncle Idriz, the child who cried and would not be consoled all those years ago when my mother was a young wife with her hand on the bridle of a great white horse. Concerned about what his family would eat after the evacuation of Prishtinë, he returned to his home for food. There he was picked off in his doorway by a sniper.

My ten days in Kosova passed very quickly and I was aware that when I returned again people I loved might be gone. It felt as if the very blood in my veins had dried up.

By now Clare and I, and by extension the interpreters, had established a good working relationship. We joined the producer Kim Robertson, in partnership with Education Services, for a period of three months leading up to Teachers' Day, an Albanian festival. This we used to present aspects of Albanian culture to teachers who were working with the children. My knowledge and use of English were much advanced by this project, and a network of colleagues and friends had begun to emerge. I went on to teach Primaries One, Two and Three of the Supplementary Albanian Language School on Saturday and Sunday mornings.

In the course of this year my father died. It broke my heart that I could not return for the funeral, but my mother and family understood that I had to wait for travel documents.

My final memories of Dad are from that first return to Gjilan. Still upright, active, he looked tired. I did not witness his final decline. Always when I return I feel he will somehow appear. He was a great husband, father, and head of the family. He had been a great policeman.

Our area at Red Road had a Community Police force. These were normal police officers who were learning very quickly and willingly about the special condition of the Albanians and, through us, of other refugees and asylum seekers. Already they understood that their uniforms were deeply alarming to us. Uniforms, badges and batons were associated with horrific, State-sanctioned violence.

For years, to some extent to this day, my sons would avoid policemen in uniforms. I too sometimes feel this shudder although I work closely with many of them and understand their inherent decency. It is not only uniforms. If a jet plane should pass unexpectedly, or if a truck start up, it is not unusual for us to check that it is not an attack.

My oldest son was invited to speak through his interpreter to a group of these police officers and this he did, describing the circumstances of his life and our reasons for being here. In the audience was another person about to enter our lives, particularly mine, and bring changes for the better.

Dr Elinor Kelly was a lecturer at the University of Glasgow, who lived in the city's West End. For twelve years she had worked with the police on sectarianism and had now turned to the problems that were arriving with the new waves of asylum seekers. It was she who had organised this training event and when my son finished answering questions she approached him. 'How good it would be to meet your parents,' she said.

Soon she visited us in our home and, for the first time in a long time, I was able to offer normal hospitality to a new friend. The boys' command of English was improving rapidly, more rapidly than their parents, so they were able to help with translations when required.

Elinor arrived with flowers and that day we entered a conversation that began with Kosova and continues, still, with discussions on asylum seekers from all over the world. It covers the challenges of language, religion, diet, education, politics, all aspects of culture, the meaning of integration. If we say we entered it that night, rather then began it, we recognise that integration has no beginning and will have no end.

Elinor's friendship has been both warm and practical and continued even after she left her university post. She continued to visit us and we her. She even visited us at New Year, the great Scottish celebration. At one point, when we thought my son's fiancé might arrive soon, she offered her flat to the young couple. Through her we met Janet Andrew, a former councillor for Maryhill, who made regular befriending visits with Elinor to the detention centre at Dungavel.

One day I received a call from Elinor. 'Rema, there is an Albanian gypsy woman here. She won't stop crying and no one can get through to her. Will you help?'

Of course I was more than willing. Elinor picked me up in her car and I went to see the woman. She was frightened and stricken by grief. We did what we could but the poor woman was eventually sent back to Albania. This was the first of a long series of befriending visits I was to make to the detention centre. These visits were extraordinarily demanding emotionally because there was so little hope to be offered. At the same time though, I continued in voluntary work with youths and recharged myself with the emotional uplift.

After about a year, when our leave to stay was coming to an end, the Home Office announced that the cancer sufferers among Albanian refugees would be allowed to stay permanently. It felt as if the decision had been made for us.

The boys progressed astonishingly well in their studies, gaining As and Bs in their Highers. Much of this was due to their teachers and interpreters, but it is also true that refugees such as us, treated as graciously as we were, are grateful and keen to repay the trust that has been put in us. They applied themselves and worked hard. All opportunities that were put before them they looked into. This included the Scout movement. It was with this organisation they went to the international rally at Auchengillan, on the edge of the Highlands, and I reported from there for Radio 21.

Scouts from fifteen different countries lived together for the weekend in a tented community very different from Stankovec Two, each tent flying its little flag to show which country was represented. Our boys flew the Albanian flag. It might seem a small thing to those who can take this aspect of their identity, and the right to declare it, for granted. It may even seem a backward step to those who view all aspects of nationhood in a poor light. For us though, it was an open declaration of 'what we are' that would have cost us our lives in our own country.

I continued to take such work as I could and found that I was discovering new ways for myself that were more than simply occupying my mind and providing some kind of income.

With others I wrote a drama entitled *Freedom* that was presented in Glasgow City Chambers by Albanian children. Then I volunteered for a one year project, again with Albanian women, echoing Sherife's commitment to the Women's Movement. On Refugee Day 2001, in Edinburgh, I assisted with an exhibition of work from different cultures. Like the Dungavel befriendings this extended my interest beyond the Albanian refugees. In 2002, with the British Trust for Conservation Volunteers I taught women how to create a better ambience in their homes for next to no cost. A momentum was gathering in my life.

The three of us, Elinor, Janet and I, sat in Janet's kitchen one day and I mentioned that a post was coming up in the Dumbarton Road Corridor Youth Health Project. 'I'd love to work there but I am really quite nervous about the interview,' I said.

Both of them laughed. 'Well, that's easily solved,' they agreed.

We went through to Janet's living room and to my

embarrassment, which made them laugh even more, they put a chair out into the middle of the floor and instructed me to sit. They placed two other chairs facing it and set about asking me all kinds of questions about my working life.

'Now, let's see, Mrs Sherifi, what was your experience of work before arriving in this country?' They pretended to be very formal and I felt I had never had such an intrusive experience before. When I was later interviewed by strangers it was almost relaxed in comparison. I began early in 2003 and, here, the arts and crafts skills that had come down to me from my mother really came into play.

I was paid for nine or, at most, ten hours a week. It was not enough, neither for the needs of the project nor to provide an adequate income. I enjoyed it though, and felt it was worthwhile. About the time it ended an advert appeared for the job in Lincoln Avenue and I successfully applied for that as well.

In March 2004 another two glands were removed and again found to be benign. This was a relief to us all and re-emphasised the wisdom of remaining. I now applied for a full-time post with the Maryhill Integration Network.

I thought I had no great hope of getting the job when I went to the interview as there were over sixty applications, but that same day I received a call from our chair, Mae Smith. 'Mrs Sherifi, I am delighted to say you have been successful in your application. Are you still willing to accept the job? We were very impressed by your interview.'

FRAMEWORK FOR DIALOGUE

Working steadily in the office all afternoon, Sharon and I have failed to notice how late it has become.

Before we know it it's time to make our way down the main road and into what used to be a local school for tonight's Framework for Dialogue meeting. Like so many buildings of its time its structure has long outlasted its function. Children are educated in more modern accommodation now, warmer and more spacious. These sandstone walls that have seen generations pass are at least a hundred years old and look good for another hundred. They were built to last. So, the place needs a new function, to serve the community in other ways and the asylum seekers are part of that.

The room has a high ceiling and bare walls. There are a few chairs around, and tables arranged in the middle so that participants can get up and walk around if they so wish. The asylum seekers assemble, drifting in as circumstances and public transport allow and, in a downstairs room, the crèche we organise for these events grows busier.

An early arrival is Kifajet, from Azerbaijan, whose daughter, Arzu, brought the house down at the Refugee Week Celebration. Heather is already here, seated at the other side of the table beside a group of four women and an older man from Pakistan. The man has a trim white beard, he is calm, wise looking and thoughtful. Nuna arrives and she and Kifajet hug and sit down and talk together in Russian, their common language. We have a substantial group of women from West and Central Africa, Charlotte among them. Ivory Coast is represented, as are Rwanda and Uganda.

Arriving at the same time are Maysa the Arabic translator and

Maryam who translates into Farsi. Both are young professional women, smartly dressed, and they are great friends. Once I introduced a visitor to Maysa and he asked, 'Farsi? Is that what I would call Parsee?', and Maysa, who is from Iran, replied, 'That's right, and we were all right until Maryam arrived and changed it because they have no letter "p" in Iraq.' And the man asked, 'What about that long and terrible war your two countries fought – shouldn't you be enemies?' To which they replied, 'Oh yes, we absolutely hate each other', and immediately hugged one another.

Maysa will translate for a group that is mostly men. Abdul from Morocco is here, as is Mohammad from Egypt. Maryam will translate for a small group that includes Sevana and Mahmood Farzan. Mahmood is one of the two poets and storytellers we have among us.

My own role is to support the members of this project, to build their confidence and help them achieve stability, safety and integration at community and citywide levels. In this I work closely with Margaret who is seated not far from me. One of Maryhill Integration Network's first volunteers, she is a committed member of the Framework for Dialogue group. Margaret makes herself available to asylum seekers round the clock, assisting at the most critical junctures of their experience, when they are destitute, detained and in danger of deportation. Her presence undoubtedly strengthens the group.

The co-workers who convene the meetings work on a rota basis and tonight Community Worker C draws us together and welcomes us and makes a start. Unusually, Colin, the representative from the Scottish Refugee Council, cannot be here. Tonight's agenda covers most of the issues that face asylum seekers: asylum policy, legal complexities, and all the normal problems of destitution when they are compounded by legal barriers to earning. Not least are detention and the threat of deportation.

Over thirty refugee organisations are working closely to represent the views of asylum seekers and refugees to government at both UK and Scotland level, and to the other large scale agencies that affect their lives. By these means we attempt to influence their policies and practices and we lobby those responsible for the conditions they live under.

Before we begin though, C hands a number of sealed brown envelopes to some of the participants. In this she is discrete but open, for within this group there is no shame in poverty. The asylum seekers have to attend Immigration every week and the envelopes contain small amounts of money to help them meet this obligation – bus fares. One of the envelopes goes to a woman seated close to me. She opens it below the table and spills the coins into her hand.

How expressive her hand is; its many muscles perform miracles of dexterity. It holds the coins below the table and turns them as the eye peers into the shadow to read the unfamiliar symbols printed around the rim. The thumb pushes them across the palm, turns them and rearranges them so she can examine each one individually. When the miraculous hand closes on them again, there is something that arrests me in the quality of its holding.

It is not the grasp of a miser, although her grip on these few coins is a secure one. Rather it is the holding of a woman who must make one pound do the work of not just two but three or even four. She has responsibilities elsewhere; she is a mother. She has choices to make. What is the best use of this money? If she walks to Immigration can she use it in some better way? She might add this small sum to other small sums and spend it on food, clothing or warmth, as so many have done before. Is it enough? The hand says, probably not, but it will have to do. It places the coins in her coat pocket and, from time to time, pats them for reassurance.

Amel, who appeared in *The Flats*, is this group's delegate with the Refugee Policy Forum. After our last meeting she met with the new Director of Immigration for Scotland and we are all anxious to hear what she has to say. C introduces her and, as she does, our orchestra strikes up. Not only are the two professional interpreters speaking, but also one member of each group, putting down a ground note of quiet voices that the speaker can surmount at a normal volume. Simultaneously translating as they are I cannot make out just what any of them is saying unless I take my focus away from the main speaker, from Amel's unwavering contralto. Instead I hear their musical qualities.

From the African group comes a rich timbre that seems to support all the other sounds. Maryam and Maysa speak more quickly and in a higher pitch than the Africans, and the Pakistani voice has a swing to it that will probably go unnoticed by its close listeners. The two Russian speakers, I know, are fluent English speakers, so they will be commenting rather than translating. All the voices together have a whispering oceanic unity.

Amel says: 'Six of us from the Refugee Policy Forum met him in his office at the Reporting Centre.' In her hand she has four pages of carefully typed agenda and other notes with her own hand-written comments that she refers to as she speaks.

The Pakistani voice asks for copies of the agenda and notes. There is only one copy but it is no difficult matter for Amel to recite the topics, housing and the provision of health care, treatment of children, detention and removal of failed asylum seekers. These last issues are her point of entry.

'First we brought to his attention how awful it is for the asylum seekers to be detained in public, whether it is at the Reporting Centre or in dawn raids on homes. It affects those of us who are not targeted even on this occasion. Of course we know we are all targets eventually so, really, it is terror. We see this horrible scene in front of us, we see the people struggling for their lives and we hear the cries of the children. I told him, "I have been really shocked. My heart was beating because I thought they had come for us – but, how are we to feel when it is for someone else, our neighbour? Should we be relieved?" Our Scottish neighbours are also affected. They come to their windows but what can they do? This is the Government we are talking about. The whole community is affected.'

The woman who translates for the Pakistani group asks, 'What did he say?'

'Nothing.'

'He knows all this very well,' says another voice. 'These procedures will not change. This country talks continually of human rights but they do not apply to us.'

'It is like a war on asylum seekers,' says a third voice, this time through a translator. 'It is like a slow war that destroys by an accumulation of blows, some small, some very painful. No one can rest. No one can sleep.'

'Perhaps this next thing can change,' Amel says, 'since it is procedural. We complained about having to go to the Reporting Centre every week. "Why do we have to report?" I asked. "So we can remain in contact," he says. "So we can exchange information."

'I told him that the procedures are humiliating. We go through the metal-detector frame as at the airport and if any noise is made, because someone has forgotten a key or something, we must go through again. We have to put everything in a box to be examined. Even the children must go through. And then the same thing happens with the hand-held machine being run all over us. The pregnant women are afraid for their unborn babies because they go through this every week. Two times they receive these rays every week.'

'What about the compensation?' someone asks, referring to a measure that was introduced about a year before this meeting. These days the asylum seekers are offered three thousand pounds to return voluntarily to their countries of origin. They are given five hundred pounds at the airport and, the idea is, they get the rest when they begin a business back there among the terrorists, or under the government of oppression, or in the starvation camps they fled from before. All they have to do is make their claim through the British Embassy.

'This offer is still in place.'

Zahra is a strong-minded woman and an effective activist for the whole of her local community, whatever their skin colour or religion. She has a practical outlook and is well accustomed to using direct no-nonsense speech. When asked where she comes from she usually answers, 'From Glasgow. Glasgow is my home.' Asked where she originates she replies, 'Uganda'.

'What is this?' she asks angrily. 'Do they not know that our lives are here now? This is where they put us. It is not that we had any choice, but we have embraced this city and made our new lives here. Three thousand pounds to return to what they call our "home"! This is our home! Is that to cover the funeral?

Do they think we escaped from nothing, for no reason?'

Nuna leans forward in her seat and asks, 'That is the price they put on a bullet? Why are they so desperate that we should leave?'

Speaking through Maysa one of the Arab men suggests, 'We have heard that more asylum seekers arrive all the time. Perhaps they need the space, our homes, to give them accommodation.'

Maryam leans across to a woman who whispers in her ear. 'They will have done their sums,' she translates. 'They know what it will cost for each of us for so long. That is where this figure comes from.'

Nuna will have none of this. 'Then why not accept us?' she asks. 'That is the answer. We can work, earn. Then we will be off of their hands and there will be room for others if that is what they want.'

'This man,' asks Zahra, 'this new Director, how long has he been with Immigration?'

Amel consults her notes. 'Since 1974,' she says, 'but he is new to Glasgow.'

'1974 is before I was even born,' says Zahra. 'Does he not know that you leave home and family? You run and you do not go back.'

To go back means interrogation, possibly imprisonment and torture. It could mean death. Certainly it would mean the death of the life created here, in difficult circumstances, through many years of anxiety and hope.

Now, it is growing dark outside. I interrupt proceedings by appealing to our convenor. 'As you know it is Ramadan. This is the time of day when observers may break their fast and I suggest we now do that.'

She agrees and one of the Pakistani women brings round a tray of dates. One of the Middle Eastern women has baked a lemon sponge and that too is passed around. Soon tea and coffee are made and we have broken into small groups of a different kind, each one chattering as informally as any such group among the host community would speak and about much the same things – food, clothing, children, practical everyday matters laced with humour.

When we reconvene, Mahmood, who is a deeply spiritual man, suggests that next time we should meet slightly later. It will still be Ramadan and this lengthy interruption to proceedings will be repeated if we meet early.

So now we must speak about the ordering of our meeting rather than its content. In this we are no different, I suppose, from the United Nations. One problem in starting later, I point out, is that it will take the meeting's end to a still later hour and the children in the crèche will become more tired.

True enough, someone points out, but the days grow shorter as the year grows older. Next time sunset will be slightly earlier and that will mean an earlier break in proceedings. Will a short first session be worthwhile? C points out that, by Council policy, she is obliged to have a break of her own between her normal office hours and restart. This pushes our start time later again. The problem is intractable. We agree to meet half an hour earlier next time and return to our present agenda.

Now we have to discuss the topics for Amel's next meeting with the Director of Immigration and the evidence we propose to submit about the treatment of children in detention, destitution and deportation.

Everyone is agreed the Framework for Dialogue meetings are

important. They help the asylum seekers to work out common ground where it is possible, and to clear their thinking on any given issue when it is not. Just as important though, is propelling their discussions outwards to a wider circle that will include whoever among the host community will listen, to the media and to politicians.

It is amazing how this group has developed since its beginning, becoming increasingly motivated, enthusiastic, involved and creative. We recently published the latest issue of our Newsletter, 'News from Friends'. The success of its launch at Maryhill Community Halls resulted from good teamwork between asylum seekers and refugees, organising bodies and volunteers and the members of the Framework for Dialogue group.

The people in the audience were from many different backgrounds as well as the local community, and they appreciated the presence of Patricia Ferguson MSP who agreed, 'Through creative initiatives Maryhill Integration Network have led the way in building bridges between asylum seekers and the people they live among. The government and the people have to be informed.'

Most of the asylum seekers are ready to speak although some, because of their condition, cannot. Four have bravely agreed to be interviewed by me about their experiences. All of their stories are different but perhaps they can give some idea of what normal human beings are capable of when placed in extraordinary circumstances, and also illustrate what are normal circumstances for them. Knowing them as well as I do I understand they do not look for pity. What they seek is acceptance and opportunity.

Now the hour has grown late, or late enough for the children downstairs in the crèche. Their requirement to be taken home before they become exhausted overrules proceedings and the asylum seekers leave as they arrived, in ones and twos and small groups. Kifajet goes down to pick up Arzu and Nuna goes for Artur. Charlotte also leaves because little David will be getting tired and it is time for bed. Then there is a flush of departures as the African and Pakistani and Middle Eastern women leave together. The men, who are older, tend to stay a bit longer before heading home.

Community Worker C, Maryam, Maysa and I tidy up; there are dishes to be washed and put away and no one else is going to do it. Through the open door I see that some of the women have paused at the top of the stairs, still talking, happy, one of them with her hand placed securely in her pocket. Like me they feel that something has been achieved. Each time we meet and agree, and then communicate somehow with officials, with government, best of all with the people, we move forward by some small increment. They have their voices, and in a fortnight will return to our small United Nations of poverty and hope.

NEWS FROM FRIENDS
Charlotte

Charlotte completes today's guitar lesson with Ian about the same time as I finish work and so we are able to speak.

She is a young woman from West Africa, wearing a smart skirt and blouse. She has reddish streaks in her hair that subtly complement the colour of her skin. Since meeting her I have been impressed by her strength of mind and confidence. She is a woman well able to speak her mind.

'I am from Ivory Coast,' she says, 'and have been here for four years. I came to study in London just before the war broke out. I left my older boy, Joel Prudence, with my husband, my father and step-mother. At the time he was nine years of age.'

'What was your situation there, Charlotte? I mean, were you well off?'

'My husband was an engineer and had a good job. My father was a retired civil servant but he also had farms. Ivory Coast is the world's leading grower of cocoa. This is what we did although he also had fruit farms. So yes, I would say we were well off. We were all happy that I should leave at the time because it was to a good end.

'It was my uncle who reached a business arrangement with some English-speaking Canadians. He made an investment and it was felt I should improve my English. That is really why I went to London to study, to improve as quickly as possible. At that time I was working in the Bank. I gave up that job to come here, enrolling for one year. Very soon I discovered I was pregnant again and this was good news for a couple who very much wanted a second child.'

'Is Ivory Coast a rich country?' I ask.

She thinks about this carefully before answering. 'Most people are poor, although the country is very productive. So, in that sense yes. France still has a lot of control over the country, although Ivory Coast is independent. There are still French troops stationed there. When the war broke out they did nothing. On the northern side and in the central part of Ivory Coast is where the rebels are. On the other side are the government troops and in between the French. The rebels do what they like.'

'Conditions were getting worse when you left?'

'No, but you have to understand what it was like in Ivory Coast even before the new president took over.'

'Was it a democracy, Charlotte?'

Again she thinks carefully before answering and I feel she is nervous about saying anything that might show her country in a poor light. But soon she is in her stride.

'I have to say that democracy is not strong in Ivory Coast. We have law but corruption is everywhere. Crime levels were terrible. There was stealing and rape. If you went out wearing jewellery the gangsters might stop you and take it. There was a lot of abuse, particularly when Robert Guei took over. He was a senior military officer when he succeeded in a coup and came to power in 2000. His soldiers abused a lot of people without being punished. They could shoot you dead and nothing would be done. At most there would be some report but then nothing would be done. Gangsters were everywhere. If you took out your mobile phone on the street it would be snatched from your ear.'

'What about freedom of speech?'

'You could not express your mind. To do so meant you would go to prison, or even be killed. When I was a student this was what we wanted, to speak out, but the government had a spy in the university. A very bad man, he was open about what he did. He would rape the women also. No one would challenge him and many, many women suffered.'

'Was there an opposition?'

'Not really. My first political activity was to be a member of FESCI, *Federation des Etudiants, Cote D'Ivoire*. It is still going, in spite of everything. If it had not been for the war I would be back there working for real freedom with my colleagues.'

'But that was not to be, Charlotte. What happened?'

'The war was very sudden. There was no warning. I had been here only four months when the rebels attacked our town. They took over the city and started killing people and the things they did were horrible. You can see it on the web sites. They cut throats. They beat people to death. They cut open the pregnant women and took out their babies and threw them aside.'

At this point I remember Prapashticë and Keqekollë and understand the repetition of atrocity. I understand that the debasement of men will find the same crimes to commit over and over. The worst things that men can do will be repeated precisely because they are the worst things.

'I was so shocked. I didn't know what was happening to my family until Dad contacted me on the mobile phone. He had been accused of being involved with the rebels and at the same time accused by the rebels of being against them. "Do not come back," he said. "I am sure we will die today but be strong and blessed where you are." Then the phone went dead and I could not get through to him when I tried. I tried to call my husband but again could not get through. This was the last I heard from any of my family. They may be alive or dead, I do not know.

'People fled, they simply left everything and everyone and fled. Each person had to go in his own way. There was no question of getting together to resist. The rebels were well armed and knew what they were doing. All our leaders fled and many of them are now in London. The French soldiers did nothing. So, what are they for?

'Since then I have received anonymous death threats and have been admitted several times for depression. I was living in fear of being killed at any time. When I became an asylum seeker I was brought here to Glasgow, separated from friends who were helping me. My right to travel was taken away as was my right to work. My freedom was taken away and I became a beggar. My worries doubled on that day, worries about being sent back, about detention, all added to the pain of my missing family.'

'You've heard nothing of them?'

'Yes I have, but nothing definite. A friend of mine has a friend who lived near us. This person managed to escape and we spoke on the phone. The rebels' first attack was near the airport and the military base so this was the point of greatest surprise. Our home was in this area so it makes it even less likely they have survived. They killed approximately five hundred people that day. This friend was kind. She said, "I can't guarantee they are alive." Since then I have tried everything I can think of, but especially the Red Cross. After one and a half years they gave me a report about someone resembling my son in the camp at Abidjan, on Ivory Coast's border with Ghana. I understand a lady took the boy with her, but I have heard no more.'

We are silent for a time, Charlotte and I. People flee to save themselves because survival is first. You can do nothing for your loved ones if you are dead. They stay away for the same reasons, and now Charlotte has David to look after. Sometimes people never meet again. They never learn if their loved ones have survived. I think of Grandmother Hamide and her own mother after the massacre at Prapashticë, and my parents when we left them in Gjilan. Beside those memories I recall my own feelings after our border crossing into Macedonia.

Charlotte continues with her eyes closed and her head lowered but this time she is not speaking to me. I can hardly hear her.

'There is no pain,' she says, 'that can be compared to the pain of a woman who has given birth to a child who has grown enough to call her *Maman*, who has felt the joy of breastfeeding and seen the love in her child's eyes and smile, who has been used to kisses and hugs when she comes back from work, who didn't hear any "bye-bye" from the child or him saying, "Mum, I'm going", or any complaint of pain when suddenly all around her becomes silence.'

I have no words to place inside this silence. None can make a difference.

'Charlotte?'

She is crying now. It is time to bring the interview to an end.

'What about the boy in Abidjan?' I ask. 'There may still be hope.'

'I am in touch with Red Cross Ivory Coast all the time,' she answers. 'But I have never managed to speak with him. People are watching for my son all along the border but we have never been in touch. I no longer believe that was my son. Many people have left their children behind and I no longer believe it was him'.

Nuna

Tonight at the Drop-In we have a rehearsal of the dance theatre work, *To Glasgow with Love*.

Natasha, a professional dancer, takes the group with a view to breaking down barriers, providing exercise and taking the asylum seekers' minds off their problems. There is another end that is also very important though. It allows them to show some of the talents and commitment they bring to the city.

The asylum seekers are of both sexes although mostly women, all ages and different fitness levels. People are here from Armenia, Iran, Azerbaijan, Brazil and the host community. Like aerobic exercisers everywhere they wear loose trousers and tee shirts. Most dance in their bare feet. Two of the older women wear long black dresses, elegant but leaving room to move. Among us all one stands out.

Nuna wears a Nike leotard and half length trousers and dances with uncanny coordination. Feet, legs, arms and hands, head, all move fluidly together. She has a different kind of fitness from Natasha, whose movements are catlike and effortless. Nuna bends and pirouettes, leans and touches the floor without giving any sense of effort, but makes no attempt to disguise the physical power in her compact frame.

She and I have become close friends since she and her little boy, Artur, arrived. She is a great support to me in my work. She is a naturally modest woman, and has a level-headed perspective on the achievements of her earlier life. Not everyone knows what I know, that she was seven times figure skating champion of Eastern Europe. Anyone can see that she is operating well within her capabilities. She recognises that this is for fun, not competition.

Early in the evening, after we are warmed up, Natasha asks each of us to come forward to improvise a dance, or perhaps dance in their national style. The others are to copy afterwards.

First Sharon goes through part of her aerobic routine, then a woman of Irish background jigs with her arms at her sides. A Scottish man lifts his arms in the air and does an improvised Highland Fling. Nuna steps forward and adopts a posture with one leg behind the other and her arms outstretched. She leaps from a standing start, turning one and a half times in the air to land gracefully and silently, still smiling. I follow all these with the same gliding motion and circular hand movements I made with Sherife and my friends on the day before my wedding in Gjilan. The other dancers are more successful copying me than they are Nuna.

When we are done and the others are leaving she agrees to speak with me while Sharon looks after her three-year-old son, Artur.

'Armenia is a small country so, the fact is, I was quite famous,' she tells me. 'Eventually though, because of the gangsters who have always run the country I fled with my brother. I was pregnant with Artur but I had to leave my two sons and my daughter behind. I don't want to go into that.'

'Then don't,' I tell her.

'We paid some Russians to take us away and eventually we arrived here. It is a terrible place Artur and I stay. There is much drink, drugs. People fight each other. The children are like this too and I am afraid for Artur that he will become like them.

'Around our flats are people who take drink and drugs every day. When they speak I tell them we want no part of what they do. Nearby there was a murder. At that time I was very frightened and wouldn't come out. I was depressed. My only help was Terry White. Did you know him?'

'Yes.'

Terry White was an older man, about seventy years of age. He would involve himself with some of the asylum seekers from time to time. I did not know him well.

'I'm sorry,' Nuna goes on, 'but he died of cancer some months ago. When we first came to the Parish Church a friend of his visited the Group and spoke with me. His name was David and he was about the same age. I had no English so we spoke with signs. When he learned I speak Russian as well as Armenian he contacted Terry who was a professor of Russian. He and his wife and daughter and granddaughter became my friends. I have to say I have very good Scottish friends. Terry's daughter meets Artur and me every week and takes us to the Safari Park at Loch Lomond, to the ice rink, nice places to eat. You know, we are normal people, we need to go to nice places and meet other normal people.'

'I understand,' I tell her. 'Normal people who want to live normal lives.'

'Terry would call me every day and now he is gone his family do the same. "How is your case going?" they ask. "Have you been sent any papers?" Whenever Immigration would send me one of their official letters, or the lawyer I was assigned would write, Terry would translate for me. He would ask how I wanted to reply and he would write for me. He wrote to the Home Office asking if I could stay.'

'That's wonderful. Were you able to repay him in any way?'

'I asked him to be Artur's godfather. He thought about this very deeply and discussed it with Mrs White. In the end he said, first, his wife is not of the church and, second, he was too old to do it properly. He would be dead before Artur was grown. I think he knew about his health. I also taught his grand-daughter to skate at Stirling Ice Rink. At the same time I taught Artur and that is where I met the skating people of Scotland. They recognised me for what I am and I know they wanted my coaching talents. They wrote to the Home Office.'

'Have you any news about your case, Nuna?'

'Nothing, I am still asylum seeker.'

'And that means you still do not have the right to work.'

She puts both hands on the table in front of her and half closes them as if there is something of vital importance that must be grasped and offered.

'All my life I have worked. From birth I was given this special talent and I have worked with it as best I can. I have been seven times champion. Now, although I am not old, I could no longer skate at that level. It is time to coach but I cannot do it because I am asylum seeker. I would work but the Home Office will not let me. I tried and they would not let me. I can show them my papers, many qualifications, but as long as I have no status I cannot work in this field.'

'This is a very great waste.'

'Yes, and not only for me but for ...' She points across to our little stage at the end of the hall where Artur is in very serious conversation with Sharon. '... for Artur and for Scottish skating. He is exceptional. At three years he is recognised for his talent. He could be a champion for Scotland. When I heard about the London Olympics I thought, "Yes!" My dream is to coach a champion for Scotland, to win the medals there in London. How wonderful that would be. As it is I can do nothing but wait and try to survive. I feel like a young pensioner. I miss the full life I had before, the life that only comes through work.'

'Will you try again to get your status? Or will you simply wait and do nothing?'

'I will do what I can to live well and not simply be helpless, but I will not write again to the Home Office. I am afraid they will simply say, "Go away!" It would be the easiest answer for them.'

'Many asylum seekers have this fear,' I tell her. 'They do not want to provoke a rejection.' Instinctively I change direction. 'You dress well.'

She smiles at this. 'People give me gifts,' she says. 'I do not like to ask, to be a beggar, but my good Scottish friends understand. I get eighty pounds per week and it is not enough to live on. There is food, phone bills, bus fares, otherwise all goes on Artur. He wants, you know, as other little boys want. He doesn't understand why he can't have the things he sees on television. I do not go into toy shops any more. It is more important that he eats well.

'You ask if I would go to work? Yes, I would work to give him these things. I tell people about the gifts and they say, "Is not so bad. We take gifts also." I say, "You choose. It is not the same. I cannot work and make money to pay for ordinary basic things you take for granted. It is not allowed." All the time this is what I want; to teach skating at high level and to live in nice, safe place and earn enough to buy what is necessary.'

'But you have another dream, Nuna? I believe you are still in contact with your older children.'

She nods, speaking thoughtfully and with consideration, also with the reluctance that comes with extreme emotional pain. 'When I can afford it I call them at my mother's home. That is where they live. I try to speak with them every week. Sometimes the White family help with money and sometimes a new friend I met through them. Dr Richard is a doctor of languages. He is seventy-six years old and does for Artur and me many of the things Terry did. I do not want to be a beggar but how can I refuse this? I have a son, eighteen, a daughter, seventeen, and another son, fourteen. There was a miscarriage. You do not forget. How can you forget? I must speak to them when I can. The nights are worst. I cannot sleep for thinking about them.'

'Usually you do not let it show.'

'From three years old, Artur's age, I have been acting. Ice is my element. Yes, my other dream is that they join me here. I cannot go back. It is unthinkable, but every day I remember my children and miss them. I miss how they smell and the smoothness of their skin. You know I like to bake, Rema? I miss things like baking cakes for them, small things like that, and buying them gifts.

'Perhaps someday they can come here. I do not know how or when but I long for that day. These are my dreams, to live here freely with my children, and with enough, and to work with great skaters and win those medals for my new country.'

Rahim

The man sitting opposite me is slim, dark skinned and good looking, fifty years of age.

He sits upright with legs crossed and his shoulders drawn rather together. He has the long, slender fingers of a musician and already I know that he also writes poetry and stories for both adults and children. This is an activity he has turned to in recent years. Introducing himself as Rahim he goes into his story.

'You need to be with your children and be together. You ask me what would happen if I went back and I tell you I cannot go back or I would never see them again. There are other reasons, the reasons we left in the first place, but the main reason – now – is my children.'

'What was your job?' I ask.

'I was a civil engineer.'

'You built roads, water works?'

'I worked on autobahns, yes, but mostly buildings. There was a new town built in the south by the gas company. For a long time I worked there. I did road works, put down bitumen road base, asphalt surfacing, these things.'

'You're a married man?'

'Yes, with two boys and one girl. We fled together to London, partly for religious reasons, partly political. That was six years ago. From London they sent us to Glasgow, to the flats at Red Road. Conditions were bad. All around us was drink, drugs, fighting. Elsewhere in Glasgow an asylum seeker was murdered. Others were attacked with knives, broken bottles or stones. We were surprised at what we found and at first I thought this was normal in Scotland. I thought everyone behaved in this way. Later I realised it wasn't a typical place. Many who lived there had problems. People sat on the stairs and injected drugs. They drank from bottles. The stairs also smelled bad. You could not even walk there. You understand what I mean?'

'Yes.'

'We were in a bad position. People who had no education or culture looked down on us, people who have probably never worked.'

'Looked down on you?'

'Not just neighbours, people such as teachers. Let me give an example. I was at aromatherapy class, learning a skill. There were twelve of us and I was the only foreigner. Teacher wanted to put on a language CD but was busy and looked to me to do it because I was closest. Can you imagine teacher looking at me while speaking, wondering if I was capable of this piece of technical know-how – to put on a CD. I did not say I had equipment better than this at home. I did not say I was more capable than teacher in these ways because people do not want to hear this kind of thing from an asylum seeker.'

'All this would be very stressful. How did you and your wife react?'

'She suffered from anxiety. We had stress from neighbours, from fear of being sent back, from not having enough money because, of course, we were not allowed to work. There were things she could not cope with and I would say they changed her. People change in good ways and in bad ways. We had arguments. Increasingly they happened over small things. I did not wish to leave but by this time it had really already happened and there was no choice.'

'How long had you been in this country, Rahim?'

'It was a few months.'

'This breakdown between you didn't take long.'

'No. Things were very different from our lives before. Really, the difference was unbelievable.'

'What about work? Could you have got a job?'

'About this time I applied for a work permit, twice, but there was no response. Three months later my asylum claim was turned down.'

'So you had to move out and were living on your own. Are

you still in touch with your children?'

'Yes, I see them every week or so. Relations with them are no different as far as feelings go. Practical things are very different. For five years I have not enjoyed them growing up and going to school as a normal father would. This was at first very upsetting. It is not really better now, only I am more used to it.'

'They must miss you too.'

'Yes, they still need me. They understand this. They are glad to see me. It is in their eyes when we meet.'

'Perhaps there is some chance of getting together again. Is there divorce in your own country?'

'Of course. Let me tell you a difference though. In this country it is assumed that the children will be with the mother. Perhaps the father will have access but mostly they will stay with the mother. This is true whether she has someone else or not. In my country it is assumed they will stay with the father.'

'What was your new accommodation like?'

'Neighbours were just like before, maybe worse. It was another block of flats, six in each storey. I had problems with being alone at first. I was not used to loneliness. I had to grow my confidence as well as my knowledge. I have always been a musician but now I started to write poems and stories. I would like to write a book and get it published. This is a new ambition.'

'What do you do with your poems when you have written them?'

'Mostly I throw them away. Some I keep; the best of them.'

'Do you write in English?'

'No, in my own language, then they are translated. Perhaps some day they will be published. I believe in free expression.'

'So you were on your own, and you learned English and you wrote and your confidence began to come back. I know you also sometimes come to the Drop-In.'

'The Drop-In became very important, but that was later. Now things got worse in the flats. I mean with the building itself. One by one the neighbours left. The last of them set fire to his home and was arrested by the police. The whole storey was covered in a layer of smoke. It was a frightening experience, terrifying; but soon I was left on my own. This gave mixed feelings. On first hand they were not good neighbours. On second – can you imagine living in such a place on your own?

'Local teenagers decided the building was suitable to vandalise. They smoked, took drugs and drank at all different hours of the day and night. I reported all this. The police also reported, but nothing was done until vandals set the whole place on fire and I was fortunate to escape the flames and extreme smoke with my life. Now there was nowhere to live but in two weeks I was moved to another area.'

'Did this give a sense of permanence?'

'Two more weeks later my support was stopped and I was told to leave the flat again.'

'What did you do?'

'At the Drop-In I had made friends among the host community. They took me in and let me stay with them. I am with them now, very grateful and wishing I could contribute more. As things stand though, I cannot take gainful employment. I try not to be defeated. I continue to go to college and I continue to write. I do all kinds of activities that I am able. I have friends both among asylum seekers and within the host community. We talk across many tongues and many different experiences of life. At every opportunity I see my children.'

'And you might be sent back to your home country?'

'I could not possibly go back, but the position of a single man is more precarious than that of a woman with children, or a whole family. My children need me, you know. They miss me when I am not there. We have strong, loving relationships although I cannot live with them.'

'What is next for you, Rahim?'

'I wait. Again I have applied for status. What can I do but wait?'

'And if you get status can you look for a job?'

'This is the key to everything. With refugee status I can enter gainful employment. What happened was painful for me before, but now I am accustomed to it. I wish my wife well in whatever is to come in the rest of her life. With steady employment I can get accommodation and my children can stay with me at the weekends and holidays. Again I can participate as their father. Together we can make a home and a life. I want nothing more than to be their guide and strength and always be there for them.'

Amel

Amel has blonde streaks through her hair, carries a bag and in every way resembles a woman from the host community. I know her from a number of events she has participated in, but not well. I also know that she has recently moved into Maryhill from an area in Pollok and that she has done good work in the schools there and elsewhere.

This is the woman who performed so memorably in *The Flats*

and at Maryhill Community Hall. It doesn't take too long to establish a humorous, friendly atmosphere. To make a proper start I ask her, 'Where are you from, Amel?'

'I come from Algeria but have been here in Glasgow for five years. Before that time I had no English. Now I have put down roots here. By roots I mean my children. One was four years old when we arrived and the other was born here but he has no country. He is not Algerian. He is not Scottish or British. If you ask them where they come from they say, "Glesga", and they have Scottish accents. They have no memories from Algeria. The first one was only born there.'

I ask her what life was like in Algeria.

'There was no safety, no peace. My husband was an entrepreneur as was my father.' Amel pronounces the word 'entrepreneur' in perfectly accented French. 'Now there is no education. It used to be French education then the fundamentalists took over. Now they beat children. They beat them in the class. In my time we weren't beaten; no. They beat the children. I couldn't believe that my son would be beaten. I was studying law at university and I left for one year and had no right to go back because I am woman.'

'What about Woman?' I ask. 'How does she fare in Algeria?'

'Woman has no rights at all. She gets abused everywhere. I wouldn't say I had any trouble with my husband but most women have trouble with their husbands. The law abuses Woman. No allowed to go out alone, made to cover up. No allowed to go without husband, or brother, or father, this is the law. If she does she is gossiped about. After nine or ten at night they will take you for a prostitute and arrest you. She can't study as she might wish and what is allowed will not take her far. She is not going to get a job at what she has studied. Woman is treated like a minor, like a child. I was surprised at the law in Europe, children are first, the woman second, all people third and the man is last. My sisters were lawyers from earlier times, and I was studying law.'

'Isn't it ironic that they serve the same law that represses them,' I ask.

'They are gone now. They left before me.'

'Has your husband adapted?'

'Not bad. Is a different environment here. I would say he is open minded but he is used to something different. I am happy here. I want to stay. I set limits to my expectations.'

'What would happen if you were sent back?'

'It would be a disaster. I would be put in detention and there would be a long interrogation. They would take me for – someone who passes information?'

'A spy?'

'A spy. Even though it was not true they would stick it on me.' Amel illustrates her speech with graceful, expressive gestures of the hand. Here she presses the thumb of one into the palm of the other. 'They would stick it on me. There is torture, death. It is true I might be killed. People are killed for giving water to extremists. They knock on the door and ask for water and if it is not given they kill you. If the government find this out they kill you too. Here I am told "your country is at peace". If it is at peace why do they not go there for their holidays? It is a beautiful country, the most beautiful country in the world.'

'But that's Scotland, isn't it?' We both laugh and the intensity that has been gathering is dispelled.

'Fighters came down out of the mountains and attacked the village called Tipaza. They killed everyone. They used very sophisticated weapons.'

'Are they the same nationality as those they killed?' I ask.

'Yes! They are Islamic extremists. They kill for their kind of Islam. They practise Islam in their way; is not the way in which the prophet Muhammad or the Qur'an asks us to do it. Not to worship like them is enough.'

'Certain things happened that made you decide to leave.'

'Yes, my sisters had already gone and were living in France. We had stayed for longer because of my husband's business. He had already been visited twice by extortionists. This is one of the ways they finance their activities. When the owner of the shop two doors along was shot we decided it was only a matter of time before they came for us. They just went in, rolled down the shutters, shot him and walked away. Everyone was too frightened to speak and the police – what are the police? – they take their notes and make their report and do nothing.

'We took such money as we could but could not sell for fear of alerting the authorities. Really, we had nothing when we arrived in London. We were brought to Glasgow from there in a bus with many others from all over the world, Kosova, Afghanistan, Turkey, people who were very different from us with different languages and different clothes.'

'Was this a great relief? It was for me when we arrived.'

'I thought no more worry, no more stress, and found myself in the housing scheme.'

'This is the housing scheme on the southern edge of the City of Glasgow. It's where you stayed until you moved into this area.'

'Yes. I couldn't believe it. On the ten hour journey we had thought of freedom. We had thought of Britain as a place of civilisation. We didn't even know where Glasgow was on the map. Immigration just put us on the bus and sent us here. It was like being put on a donkey that goes where it likes. We were harassed from the day we arrived. People write on the walls. They sit on the stairs and drink alcohol. We think, "This is Great Britain?"

'All of the people looked on us coldly, but one family treated us like dirt. I nearly lost my mind. That would have been less bad. When you lose your mind you have nothing left to lose. My youngest was slow to learn to walk because of the stress, he became aggressive and I became depressed. The other was affected at school. He did poorly. I couldn't communicate with my children my head was so full of what might happen next. They were horrible. Racial abuse was endless. We were told, "Go back to your own country." They spat at us, threw dirty water at us, and they deprived us.'

'Deprived you?'

'Yes, they prevented us from going out and they swore at our guests. They ordered us to go away.'

'Did you receive any help?'

'Yes, I had drug therapy for the depression. There were times I felt I had been better off in Algeria.'

'Amel,' I say. 'In Algeria you almost lost your life. You were threatened three times. In your new home did you feel you might be killed? What was it like?'

She is thoughtful about this. It seems a fine point is about to be made. 'It was like being put over a small flame and turned and slowly roasted alive.'

'Were there other asylum seekers close by?'

'Yes, at the other side of the scheme. They had trouble too but not so bad as we got from this one family which was above us. They were horrible. It was in their faces, twisted with hate. I didn't expect to find this kind of people in UK. The police said we understand but there is nothing we can do. Just keep quiet.'

'They were right,' I say. 'If you had assaulted them, for example, you'd have been in trouble.' At this point I feel I have something important to say. 'I do not want to generalise but what I always say to asylum seekers is that you get good and bad everywhere. Someone opened this door to understanding for me and he was a Serb, a surgeon. I always say this to my boys because they do not have good memories of Serbs, only bad: good and bad are everywhere. You had bad luck, Amel.'

'It was horrible, Rema.'

'I know your experience and I know your qualities,' I tell her. 'You go into schools now and talk to children. What about their reaction to your presence and your stories, and their parents' reaction?'

'I have been visiting schools for two years. The Head Teacher of the local school invited me along. These children from the neighbourhood learn French and I tell them about where I come from and why I am here. They ask me why I speak French when I come from Algeria, although I tell them I speak Algerian as well. They don't know about one hundred and fifty years of occupation and the effect it has. Slowly, slowly, slowly you get through and they speak to their parents and then I find myself speaking to their parents also.'

'This is what happens,' I agree. 'I worked as a volunteer for four or five years in poor areas of Glasgow. They get to know you and to understand and their attitudes change. Before they know us they think we get everything free, but asylum seekers always want to work.'

'Definitely!' she exclaims. 'We want to bring what we have to the host community.'

'One of the most important things in my life is having the right to work,' I say. 'But you are already breaking down barriers, Amel. You are already volunteering.'

'Oh yes, I was working with the YMCA, writing stories with The Village Storytelling Centre, which is based in St James Parish Church in Pollok. Many Scottish people were protecting us because we were persecuted.'

'The police protected you?'

'Not the police in the first time; no. There was a dialogue group at the YMCA and I went there. We had English classes and the Framework for Dialogue. I was the only person there at the beginning.'

'Not much dialogue with just one person,' I say.

'I persuaded other asylum seekers to come along. Joining the YMCA was life changing. There I met people from The Village Storytelling Centre and I discovered I had that talent of drama, talent to write stories. I was afraid to go home after workshops though, so they didn't let me go alone. They drove me to my house and every day I would come back in a different car. Mercedes! Jaguars! The curtains twitched.'

I can't help but laugh at this.

'All of these people learned my worth, learned what I had been studying in Algeria, and through them I became involved in many things. After my experience at the primary school I suggested that we visit all the schools in Pollok. Let them meet us and judge for themselves. What is this new community? Who are the asylum seekers? I spoke to the Refugee Council and they welcomed the idea. So we started to do it. Now we are planning to go to all the high schools in Pollok. The local newspaper wrote on this. They called it awareness raising.'

'This is a strong route,' I say. 'Wonderful. What else have you done?'

'Many things; I am coordinator for black and ethnic minorities and asylum seekers with Fire and Rescue and I am a member of the Refugee Policy Forum. As a storyteller and actress I work within The Village Storytelling Group and I am a member of the Integration Network.'

'Well,' I say, 'I think we should certainly talk about the difficulties of integration but what a road you've made. Now you've told me about your life in Algeria, about why you left and your difficulties here. You've told me about your efforts at integration, which have been really successful, even impressive. But now, I understand there is a shadow hanging over you.'

'That's right. I am fighting deportation. All kinds of good reports about me and my family have been put in by people I work with, but they have not been successful. All they say is that Algeria is at peace.'

'Yes, Algeria is termed a friendly nation.'

'A friendly nation? Algeria?' Amel looks amazed at this pairing of words.

'But not to you,' I interrupt.

'I left my family in Algeria. People here have become my second family. They telephone me every day, you know. "What happened to you? Are you still here?" They support me.'

'I understand this,' I tell her. 'Whether or not you are allowed to stay has nothing to do with your contribution. You might be someone who arrives, takes things for granted, does nothing, and if conditions are right between the two countries be allowed to stay. On the other hand you might be a contributor, someone who has worked hard at integration and who fits in, someone who is valued by the host community around them, as you are, and be sent away. This will be because of larger politics that occur over your head. It has nothing to do with settlement.'

'My life begins each day at 8:00am,' Amel says. 'By that time I know my home has not been raided by Immigration and we have at least another 24 hours.'

GOING HOME

From all over Kosova they came in their thousands to honour the life of the dead president.

For all that it was early in the year and freezing they lined the streets outside our parliament. From inside they could hear sombre music playing as they waited through the night to enter and view the body. Drawing their coats and scarves more tightly around them they shuffled forward and beneath their slow-moving feet snow turned to slush and chilled them.

Among them was my brother Ismet, carrying with him the respects of our mother and the rest of the family in Gjilan, also carrying with him the respects of the Sherifi family, so far away. Like the rest of the crowd he contemplated the difficult times of our recent past, the turbulence of our longer history, and our uncertain future.

Since the day we had voted ourselves a republic, Ibrahim Rugova had been our leader. On the long dark road to freedom the light we followed was held aloft by him. His wise words held us back from actions that would have lost us the sympathy of the world. The same violent actions when we were in no way prepared would have brought about our annihilation. All this he saw in advance and his leadership took us safely through those haunted woods. His energetic counsel among the great powers, in Europe and at the United Nations, brought us recognition such as we had never known before, recognition as a people.

The time we were living in always felt like our time of greatest need. KFOR had brought an end to Serbian violence but the longer future had to be looked to. The voice of Ibrahim Rugova was more than ever required. We needed him, now more than ever, for his sanity and clear view of what is possible, for his restraint and patient determination.

Agron Bajrami, then editor of our biggest newspaper, *Koha Ditore*, wrote, 'He was the leader of the biggest party in Kosova, the strongest in the coalition government, and also head of the negotiating team. In all those positions he was an extremely important unifying factor.' It was not violence that took President Rugova from us but worries and lung cancer. He had played his part well but now he was gone.

Now a new crossroads appeared before us as negotiations were begun. In Kosova we were pessimistic about achieving progress with the Serbian authorities. We believed that the United Nations Security Council would have to impose a settlement and, that being so, hoped that the Serbian people would accept. Kosova could then be recognised internationally and we could work through to a lasting peace. The word on everyone's lips was 'independence', the destination we had identified so many years before.

Yugoslavia was no more, and with its departure old antipathies had been released and territorial claims reasserted. It was not that they had been reborn. Tito's version of Socialism had only contained them, never laid them to rest. Neither the Nationalisms of the nineteenth century that ended with the First World War, nor Fascism that ended with the Second, nor Communism that ended in my lifetime, had ever replaced them. Instead they had attached themselves to whichever form of identity, whether nationhood, religion or ideology, would best carry them on. The Balkans has never known large scale integration except by dictatorship, genocide and rape.

The criminals behind the violence one by one met their fates. First was Arkan, whose paramilitaries perpetrated so many atrocities. He suffered a gangster's death, shot three times in the back of the head by an off-duty policeman in a hotel in Belgrade. His career had begun with delinquent crime and progressed through robbery and assassination across Europe until eventually he operated at the level of genocide. Cynically he wove his family story into Serbian mythology and became a hero to some. He developed a patriotic, warrior glamour but eventually died as he had lived, as Milosevic associates often did. Biljana Plavsic, who congratulated him among the rubble of Vukovar, gave herself up. Charged with genocide, Sheshel also gave himself up.

Slobodan Milosevic was put on trial at The Hague before the International Criminal Tribunal for the Former Yugoslavia but never came fully to justice. He was found dead of a heart attack in his cell some two months after the death of Ibrahim Rugova. Political and spiritual opposites, they met their ends remarkably close in time.

Many criminals, but most notably Ratko Mladic and Radovan Karadzic, the leader of the Bosnian Serbs, remain at large at my time of writing. They must be brought to account for their deeds. If they had been faced down earlier in their careers the terrible suffering that occurred not only in Kosova, Bosnia, and Croatia, but in Serbia itself, would not have happened.

Serbia had by now returned to democratic processes and elected a new president and it seemed that everything had changed. From Glasgow I looked on with optimism until one day I came home and switched on the television news. In the shadow of the constitutional negotiations the Serbian Prime Minister, Vojislav Kostunica, had visited the monastery at Graçanicë and spoken in the same terms as had Milosevic in

1989. This time there were no stones being handed out, no riot being organised, but the message was the same. 'Kosovo always has been and always will be a part of Serbia.'

My heart sank because I had felt sure that of the choices before the negotiators, limited autonomy within the Serbian state, partition or independence, only independence had the potential to end the sequence of violence, revenge and clearance. Beyond that I had another optimistic dream, and that rests with the European community; that Kosova's independence might be contained within a borderless Europe. This Europe would be strong, united in spirit, and industrious, its peoples together under one sky.

I believe that no one has more to gain from this dream than the Serbian people themselves. In all of the recent conflicts they suffered too. As they grow back from the loss of their children into a fuller understanding of what was perpetrated in their name, grow out of the ashes of a broken economy and a damaged culture, it is vital that they grow straight and without resentment. I cannot and will not forget the good people in Belgrade who befriended us in our time of need. Nor will I forget the children's cancer ward. Independent Kosova can stand beside them, secure in the recognition of national difference and, through that, into the greater recognition of our shared humanity.

New democratic parties had been formed since the war: the Alliance for the Future of Kosova, the Party for Democratic Change, the Democratic League. The Clock Party took their name proclaiming that 'the time has come for change'. The Self-Determination League was unhappy with post-war progress and frequently demonstrated for a speedier route to independence. The KLA had also evolved with many members now enlisted in the Kosova Protection Corps, effectively a civil police force. Other former members were dedicated to the removal of mines, particularly around the Albanian border, and yet others to the rebuilding of the country's infrastructure.

There is no forgetting. How can there be? At the place where Adem Jashari and his family were killed there will soon be a memorial complex and country park. Beneath our sense of grief we understand that continuing will be a test of our resource and our worth.

Our wider family has been fortunate. Most survived and returned, and not merely survived but prospered. In a country that now has an employment rate of only around 25% and desperate underinvestment, that will take many years to rebuild even with independence and international aid, all have jobs or businesses and are thriving.

Ismet manufactures Kosovan military goods such as flags, badges and epaulettes used by both the territorial army and the police. In so doing he employs, at present, nearly thirty women. His daughter Margarita is manager of the German Bank in Gjilan and Arta worked for Oxfam and other charitable agencies before moving into her father's company. Albulena is studying fashion design in Prishtinë and Ardian is completing art studies in Vienna.

Ahmet repairs and markets mobile phones and carries out satellite dish and cable installations. He and his wife Naza and their children live in the family home with my mother. Salihe enjoys good health but inevitably grows older and less strong. Naza is what we call a real 'hard love woman', meaning her caring goes beyond mere sympathy and is practical, strong and determined. Zana and Ema also help to look after her. It is a great relief to me to know that my mother is cared for in this way and it makes my life here easier.

My other brother, Agim, has been Enterprise Development Officer for the past three years. Albert is Health and Safety Manager at the United States International Development offices in Prishtinë and his wife, Teuta, is a practising dentist. Adonis works for an American construction company and his wife has a shop selling baby clothes. Their father returned to his former post at the University of Prishtinë. Shemsi has a business importing construction materials and Afërdita continues as Secretary to the new police force. Both live with the memories of what was discovered in the police stations after the Serbian retreat.

My boys live in a different world even to the one I grew up in. In Glasgow we can use a small piece of plastic to speak with our family in Gjilan. They communicate across the world by internet. By air Kosova is now only three hours away. Their generation travels the world as no other has been able. Even their dreams are different. My boys say that, when they are successful businessmen, they will have homes in Scotland, the Highlands of Kosova, and in Turkey. I tell them to dream those dreams, nothing is more important.

All the boys have returned and made contact with their relations. The oldest even met Sejdi, Auntie Tush's son who went to Germany. They met in Ismet's house and were immediate and intimate friends and I can hardly say how the closing of this circle warmed me. I am homesick for all I lost, but I am here in Glasgow now and I am living a new life.

My experience has taught me not only to accept the changes that have occurred around me, whether or not they are the results of violence, whether or not they are illegal and unfair, but also the changes in myself. This is the key to sanity and continuation. I accept the loss of loved ones and homeland as I accept the loss of part of my body. Acceptance remakes me.

I believe in God. Most of the people I live among today are secular Christians. Some would describe themselves as agnostic or atheist but, even for them, the ground they spring from is Christian. I am a Muslim. I dress as a Westerner dresses, not using any special covering because, like them, I am a European woman. In fact, Albanians are the oldest nation in Europe.

I am as conscious and caring of my appearance as most women and make decisions on such things as hair colour and hemlines similar to any woman of my age. Probably my belief is only slightly different and the difference has been not so much determined by the religious divide as by environment and experience. Where most of the women I know have conducted their internal debate on a basis of social stability and the ideological movement through feminism, mine has taken place in the presence of tanks, the knowledge of rape, and the reality of flight.

I pass through the city without notice, yet I live where nations, religions and ideologies meet. I do this as a native of the Balkans, especially as an Albanian, and also in my work with asylum seekers and refugees.

The primary motors for any of the world's troubles may seem like hatred, intolerance and violence, but for those of us who have to flee they are fear, insecurity and pain. We have enough to contend with in what life throws at us, as both Sherife's death and Rugova's show. To add to it as we do is a madness of the human condition.

Internationally, the tide of violence rises and perhaps rushes towards some terrible conclusion we cannot yet see. All over the world whole peoples are fleeing and we are not prepared. They run from religious oppression and from territorial expansion, from disease and poverty and from environmental change. Above all they flee from violence inflicted by other human beings. Experience tells me they are more like us than different, and this likeness runs far ahead of skin colour, race and traditions.

The work we do in integration is piecemeal. We put programmes together and we seek funding. Often it is not forthcoming. Long-term planning is impossible even for the asylum seekers who are with us now. Increasing numbers, generated by increasing turbulence in the world, look for new beginnings. Their strongest emotion when they are dispersed 'without choice' into our worst housing conditions, housing stock that would otherwise lie empty, is gratitude.

Many of them are highly educated individuals of extraordinary resource, but the shock of encounter with the most deprived levels of our society is very great. People have positive notions of the country they are coming to, notions that have nothing to do with the welfare state and everything to do with a successful cultural and economic history. Time and again I hear the words, 'This is Great Britain?' With the pain of exile it can be too much. Depression is common. Marriages break down. Suicide happens. Yet this is better than what they have run from.

We work with them person to person, person to family, and we grow to love them. How could we not? When they are taken back into detention we share their fear. When their cases fail and they are sent away we suffer grief. Recently Kifayat and her husband Artur, little Arzu and her brother Michael were taken away by mistake. Mother and children were released within a few days but the father's release took much longer and those were anxious times. After twice being released from detention with her young sons Zahra has been deported back to Uganda, although Glasgow had become their home.

At the political level our easiest answer is to turn them back, as in 1939 the *St Louis* was turned and turned again until it eventually returned its cargo of Jews to the Nazis. This can be our response if we so choose. Otherwise we must show foresight and prepare. Acceptance of these lost souls will cost us little and, long term, bring us many benefits. It will increase our diversity and deepen our gene pool. It will bring us new ideas and energy and help us to further integrate into the world that is coming.

Here, above the Drop-In Café in the building that was designed so long ago by Charles Rennie Mackintosh, four square and reliable in its solidity, I continue in my work from day to day. I am one of the lucky ones in that I live in safety with my family and we are happy. All of us work, as is the nature of our people, and we talk into the night. The boys are grown and have completed their studies. My youngest son is married and his wife has at last been allowed to join us. As a mother of boys I am glad to have another woman in the house. My husband and sons have a wonderful relationship. They talk about business, sport, their shared passion, and they enjoy a drink together. In my gratitude for this I can even be a little bit jealous.

It is in the nature of things that they will leave the family home and their departures will probably come in the not too distant future. Like my sister Sherife I am of my family's first generation to marry entirely by choice. I know now I chose well.

My husband has been my rock from the day of our marriage

to the present. Through the loss of Sherife, and later my father, through the stress and surgery of breast cancer and the threat of its return, through political turmoil, through attack and flight, through that terrible journey into Macedonia, through the pain of exile and my commitment to the asylum seekers, he has been always beside me and often leading. Through him my boys know what it is to be a man.

I worry about the people of Kosova. They have terrible memories. People have lost entire families, others have loved ones still in prison or live in hope of returns that may never happen. The future cannot be built on recollections of horror or decisions made by others. I hope and pray they will recover from the past to live with their memories, but look to the future. Perhaps I ask too much, but how else can we continue? The cycle of violence must be ended somehow. After peace and justice the final necessity is the will to forgive.

Downstairs the café has emptied. The phone will not ring again tonight. I finish our plan of coming activities and now, surely, the future of the Oasis Women's Group, the Framework for Dialogue, and all those other projects will be assured. Since I began this book, both summer and autumn have passed. The sun has shifted in its arc across the sky and it is only now, much later in the day than when I began, that it falls on my geranium and my spider plant.

That reminds me, they need to be watered. They have to be tended. Somehow Kosova will come through. Somehow humanity will, I mean *our* humanity, the essence of what we are, but not without attention. It is growing dark. The asylum seekers, Charlotte, Nuna, Rahim, Amel and the rest have gone. I hope they are still with us in the morning.

APPENDIX ONE:

INTERVIEW WITH JANET ANDREWS, SECRETARY OF THE MARYHILL
INTEGRATION NETWORK AND WITH DR ELINOR KELLY

We meet at a café in the West End of Glasgow. It is late summer and the schools have opened for the new term. The streets are filled with teenage pupils and the café is busy. To hear ourselves speak we sit outside. Present are Janet Andrews, Secretary of the Maryhill Integration Network, Elinor Kelly, a freelance academic specialising in race and ethnic issues, Remzije Sherifi, of the Maryhill Integration Network, and Robert Davidson of Sandstone Press.

Janet: After I retired from teaching I became a city councillor until I stood down in 1999. After a year's 'rest', I first began my voluntary work with refugees and asylum seekers. In that way I came to know that Nick Hopkins was setting up the Maryhill Integration Network. Speaking to him I decided to become involved. When I joined I said categorically that I would not take on any official post – a decision that was abandoned in 2002 when I became Secretary. Now I continue in the post, which has grown considerably since our employment of a Development Worker – Remzije.

Elinor: I came to the city in 1992 as Senior Lecturer in Race and Ethnic Issues at the University of Glasgow, where I inherited a Strathclyde police training programme – 'Policing a Multi Racial Society'. From the start I noted a positive attitude to community policing as a principle of good policing, rather than a method to be tried when others had failed. Senior officers responded well to changes that I recommended so that we kept up to date in a fast moving field. When the Kosovars arrived under the government humanitarian programme I introduced Kosovar speakers into the police training.

It was through one of the courses that I meet Remzije's oldest son and was immediately impressed with the importance of police–asylum-seeker dialogue. Through him I met his parents, Remzije and her husband, and his brothers. We struck up a rapport in spite of the fact we had no language in common in our early days. Remzije, in particular, proved to be a marvellous communicator, able to speak from the 'inside' of her family's experiences.

I particularly wanted to involve a woman in the police courses, because someone who speaks as a wife and mother is apolitical. With a male speaker, less able to speak of the deep emotions that are stirred in trauma and exile, there tends to be more resistance from a police audience.

Remzije agreed to speak to a course group of community officers and I remember how nervous she was. Really, it went beyond nerves. She was shaking in the presence of the police.

Remzije: Remember, we had for years been policed by a hostile force who answered to no one for their indecent treatment of the public. They were able to beat and kill and frequently did. They had all the characteristics of an occupying force. It took time to break down this conditioning.

Robert: I expect your background in radio journalism helped. You had spoken to groups many times.

Remzije: Yes it did.

Janet: You also come from a police background in that your father was a senior policeman.

Remzije: That also helped. My brother Ismet has a business supplying uniforms to the new Kosova police. He is very successful and I am proud both of the success and the nature of the business. Anyway, I quickly found that Strathclyde Police are very different from the Serbs who took over our force when autonomy was removed.

Elinor: So, the Kosovars arrived and I have to say that the programme that supported them was a model of good practice. The Kosovars experienced precisely the conditions that are required if problems are to be solved as and when they arise.

Although they were housed in areas of poverty and watched warily by their neighbours they arrived to high profile political and media support for their plight. They, and their neighbours, were kept informed and were encouraged to access a locally based, on-site, project office where not only council staff but also interpreters were available. The Kosovar asylum seekers were given cash, not the hated vouchers that were introduced in later years. So, they could shop without stigma.

Education was provided not only for children in school, but also for adults in their community education classes. One of the high points of the Kosovars' first year in Glasgow was the presentation of their learning certificates in Glasgow's City Chambers.

Relations between the Kosovars and the host community were good but, remember, it was assumed to be finite. The authorities expected that most would return to Kosova. When Glasgow made a contract with the Home Office to accept hundreds more asylum seekers, the situation changed radically. The Kosovar project facilities were closed, at the very time that asylum seekers began to arrive in greater numbers, from many more countries, as families and isolated individuals.

I remember standing at Remzija's window with her and talking sadly about the consequences of the loss of support for the newcomers, and their neighbours.

Remzija: There had been assaults, persistent threatening phone calls. People, especially young people, had been targeted.

Elinor: Asylum seekers cannot settle, start to recover from the past, deal with the legal complexities of their applications, housing, health, welfare, educational and social issues if they live in fear of their neighbours.

Robert: What did the Project Office do and why was it removed?

Elinor: It provided advice. It was a focus for both the asylum seekers and their neighbours. It was removed because funding was withdrawn by the Home Office once they considered the Kosovar humanitarian programme had been completed.

Robert: Janet, as Secretary, funding is within your area of interest. Isn't this a Westminster function?

Janet: Yes, but it is a bit more complex than that. The funding for housing the asylum seekers and their health and education, initially, was part of the contract between Glasgow and the Home Office, which of course is Westminster not Holyrood. So was the subsistence paid in vouchers, which could be spent only in certain supermarkets (with no change given) and which was very stigmatising.

Whilst the Network was run solely by volunteers with the added value of two workers part-seconded from their posts, the funding issues centred on how this 'benefit' was distributed and the limitations of choice in where they could be spent. But once application was made to Glasgow City Council for a Development Worker, we were into a different funding scenario. Eventually, in 2004, funding was granted for a part-time post, and Remzije was the successful applicant. Each year, as with many other small voluntary organisations, the Network is involved in funding applications to continue the post, and additionally, for an Administrative Assistant as well.

The grants we have received from Glasgow City Council have been funds allocated by the Scottish Executive for asylum-seeker/refugee projects; now that has changed with the emergence of Communities Scotland as one of the funding bodies, and North Glasgow Community Partnership as another.

This has meant two sets of applications for the posts, and these are done on an annual basis, as well as applications to various bodies at various points throughout the year for the events organised by our Development Worker. So far, we have been fortunate in receiving funding – without it the Network could not operate in the way that it has since Remzije's appointment. Perhaps you can see why this secretary needs a secretary!

Robert: I notice when people become involved with the asylum seekers they seem to stay involved. As you say Janet, you've continued with this project for a number of years now.

Janet: That's true. It has that quality of adherence. What has been a noticeable feature to me is the involvement of the churches. Without their involvement we would not be anything like as successful.

No one could be more secular in outlook than I am. I have had little contact with church people for much of my life. Now I find many of them giving and giving, and asking nothing in return and I discover I see beyond this 'belonging to a church' and see them as human beings. It's not uniform among church members, of course. Our Treasurer is of the opinion that the Network has brought the churches in the Maryhill area closer together.

Elinor: I think I have learned a great deal about 'charity' among local Christians. The people I know do not use the word to mean 'handouts', they mean 'refuge and support to the destitute'.

Another, very important thing we have found is that church people are reliable. If they say they will do something, they will do it. The partnerships that have formed between churches and asylum seekers are strong, constant.

Robert: Has there been progress since the appointment of a Development Worker? How have things improved?

Janet: When Remzija began in post, the Network, which was run solely by volunteers, had three Drop-Ins and a Women's Group run jointly with Maryhill Community Health Partnership. At that time there was little contact with the Women's Centre in Maryhill. Now the Drop-Ins are still going strong, the Women's Group is being run entirely by the Network, since the Health Partnership lost its funding, and the Women's Centre is running courses with the Network.

She is a very creative person, and her talents have benefited not only the asylum seekers and refugees, but also local people, who have been encouraged to participate in the Integration Music Club, and to come along to our various social events, displays, trips and exhibitions. She has played a part in integrating Maryhill with Maryhill.

If you're an asylum seeker here your week could be given over to activities organised in the area, Further Education courses and the usual round of lawyers, the Home Office, medical appointments, etc. All of course, are imbued with waiting for a decision from the Home Office – a very long wait as some of our asylum seekers have been in the UK for nearly five years.

In imagining and creating these developments, and with her steady presence and reliability, Remzija is a tower of strength to both adults and children who are sometimes in a desperate condition.

INTERVIEW WITH NICK HOPKINS, CO-FOUNDER OF THE
MARYHILL INTEGRATION NETWORK

We are in the sacristy of Saint Gregory's Roman Catholic
Church, Maryhill.

Present are Nick, Remzije and Sharon of Maryhill Integration
Network, also asylum seekers Jean from Cameroon, Mahmed
from Algeria and Mahmood from Iran; Raymond, Anne, Bettie,
Marie and her granddaughter Shona, and Brother Lucas of the
Saint Gregory's congregation; and Robert Davidson of
Sandstone Press. It is a small room with many books, many
Catholic icons, and a clock. Very quickly those present separate
themselves into three different conversations.

Of these the conversation between Nick, Remzije and Robert
takes the form of an interview of Nick. After a short while they
are joined by Sharon. The subject is the founding of the
Maryhill Integration Network, its history and aims and its likely
future. Introductions are made and the conversation proceeds.

Nick: My name is Nick Hopkins, originally from Chester, and I
came here to Glasgow in 1995. Wales is my team. At the
University of Glasgow I took my second degree, a Masters in
Urban Policy. In 1998 I joined the Glasgow Council for the
Voluntary Sector as Policy Officer. Taking a job here and buying
a home I might be looked on as an economic migrant, in a way.

From early 2000 asylum seekers began arriving in Glasgow and discussions began about how best to respond to their needs. A friend of mine, Heather Voisey, did some key work pulling together a first network of agencies and people working with asylum seekers.

My own involvement began when I helped to organise a big conference in conjunction with colleagues in the Scottish Refugee Council and Positive Action in Housing. There was a huge attendance from community organisations, showing the concern that people had about the new arrivals in the city. A great number of ideas were generated, but the biggest thing was people recognising the need to coordinate and work together.

Robert: Going back to the need for coordination – what happened next?

Nick: Work began in the setting up of ten integration networks across Glasgow and I was involved in founding four of them. These were Maryhill, Pollokshaws, Gorbals, and Govan. All are still functioning. In fact all are stronger now than when they began. Here in Maryhill we began by identifying three likely drop-in venues at Maryhill Parish Church, Saint Gregory's Roman Catholic Church and at Findlay Memorial Church. The response from the congregations was fantastic! This is the sort of project that people become very quickly and enthusiastically immersed in.

We put a leaflet together in five or six languages advertising the drop-in centres, much of this done on a wing and a prayer. It was a friend of mine and his colleagues at BBC Monitoring in Reading who did the translations for us. We had to gather together the addresses of the dispersed asylum seekers without breaching the Data Protection Act; no easy matter. All this was low tech, word of mouth stuff. So was delivery; we put them through the letterboxes by hand.

Remzije: You talked about drop-in centres in the early days – what else did the Network get involved in?

Nick: We pushed the idea of cultural events to promote cultural integration. You could say we interpreted the word 'culture' pretty widely. In May 2002 the Scottish International Rugby team was due to play the Barbarians at Murrayfield in Edinburgh and they always have a certain number of charity tickets. We applied and they were really forthcoming and positive. That fine spring day we went through to Edinburgh in an open-topped bus we managed to borrow and had a fine time. In these ways we understood we had made our beginning.

Robert: Do you mind if I ask what your motivation is? I mean, it's quite obvious there is an informal, personal dimension that appears around the asylum seekers. It's apparent everywhere. You've mentioned the churches. Are you a Christian, Nick? Is this part of your Christian commitment?'

Nick: Me? I wouldn't describe myself as Christian in any formal sense. No, if anything I'm a religious agnostic. My involvement originally was a professional one but, in my time at GCVS, working with refugees and asylum seekers was by far the most invigorating, satisfying work I was involved with. Everything else seemed a wee bit pallid in comparison. When I changed employers to join the Glasgow Housing Association there was no question of becoming detached. It's not that I want to retain ownership of the work; local ownership is what's needed.

Sharon: Where else are asylum seekers dispersed to? I know Glasgow is the only city in Scotland.

Nick: Various cities in England such as Liverpool, Newcastle, Plymouth and all points in between. In Scotland only Glasgow signed the contract with the Home Office. You know, I think Glasgow really gained by doing so. The city's population has been in decline for decades. Some communities have hollowed out and there is a real issue about the number of empty homes. Highland's problem, for example, is just the opposite – not enough houses. So, the city has gained economically and socially from the arrival of new blood.

Just now you asked me about motivation and I talked about commitment and satisfaction. There are other rewards. I have friends now from all over the world, and they have all kinds of ranges of experience. For example I am close to a family from Iraqi Kurdistan. The man fought against the Saddam regime. Over the years he lost his father, his first wife and their son. Yes, he actually used a Kalashnikov in earnest. He is a very strong minded and determined individual and I have been privileged to know him. On that last point there is sometimes an illusion within the host community that all asylum seekers are weak little individuals trembling in their houses. Not so; many of them can handle themselves very well. I mean physically if necessary. Want a laugh? I was visiting one night and it was dark when I left. He wouldn't let me go down the road on my own! He insisted on accompanying me.

I have learned a huge amount from these friendships. Mahmed across there speaks to me in French. His English rapidly improves but, thanks to him, so does my French. Mahmood is a deeply spiritual man. He is a tolerant, open-minded Muslim dealing in the world of ideas and change. This did not endear him to the authorities in Iran and that is why he is here. Their loss is our gain.

Robert: My experience while working with Remzije is that the asylum seekers are quite exceptional people. So uniform is this it's remarkable.

Nick: That's correct! The children attend schools that have often been among the lower achieving establishments. But they are really shaking things up. Mostly they do extremely well. Remzije's sons are prime examples of this. In my current job one of them asked me if he could come up with something to break down the social barriers inherent in high flats as part of his final year project. He produced a masterpiece of interior design for the ground floor of a multi-storey building. Another thing is that the children of the host community also perform better. I guess they live with an example of what is possible that their parents never did.

Look, I'm going further than all this and looking into the future. Some people, soon as they can, rush off back to London, the city they have mostly come through. Many more stay. In the time it takes for their status to be granted they have put down roots. The kids are doing well at school, as we've noted. Through voluntary organisations, sometimes in other ways, they have built themselves into a workspace they can open up as soon as legality allows. They are involved in local communities and faith communities and national communities and the sum of this is that they stay. They become Glaswegians.

Robert: You've reminded me of Amel's children saying they're 'frae Glesga'. I've since heard them and it's true. Let me tell you it sounds strange to a native Glaswegian who, like me, has been away and come back. But they aren't the first immigrants to take on local colours. There have been Irish, Poles, Jews, many more, and many have done very well in a generation.

Nick: So, there is a new Glaswegian on the way, probably a new kind of European. Because they are starting with nothing they will not be cautious or afraid. They will be involved in economic activity rather than simply be job seekers. They will mix and mingle with the host population. Already there is – what will we say? – romantic interest across what might look like barriers. Difference is exciting, and this kind of thing doesn't wait for someone's status to arrive.

Remzije: This is the meaning of integration. The culture will change over the next few years and the yeast of new ideas, new international connections, new people, will work some kind of good magic that we cannot yet see. Let's strive towards it.

GLOSSARY

APC: Armoured personnel carrier.

Arkanovci: Chetnik 'special forces' loyal to Arkan.

Asylum Seeker: Someone who is waiting for their application for 'refugee status' to be assessed by the government.

Chetnik: Generic term for Serbian paramilitary fighters.

conFAB: Founded in January 2004, conFAB aims to support, develop and expand opportunities for writers of all mediums, encouraging the innovative growth of the arts of the written and spoken word across Scotland and internationally.

CSCE: The Conference on Security and Co-operation in Europe was established in 1973 and became the Organisation for Security and Cooperation in Europe on 1 January 1995. It is the world's largest security organisation, whose 'participating states span the geographical area from Vancouver to Vladivostok'.

Dispersal: In terms of the Immigration Act 1999, the condition of being an asylum seeker placed in UK accommodation on a 'no choice' basis.

Illegal Asylum Seeker: By definition there is no such thing.

KFOR: NATO's Kosova Protection Force.

KLA: Kosova Liberation Army.

LDK: Democratic League of Kosova.

LPRK: Popular Movement for the Liberation of Kosova.

MNLK: Movement for the National Liberation of Kosova.

OSCE: See CSCE above.

Refugee: Any person who has a well-grounded fear of persecution for reasons of race, religion, nationality, membership of a particular social group, or political opinion; is outside the country they belong to or normally live in; and is unwilling to return home through fear of persecution (1951 Convention on Refugees).

Status: Refugee status as granted by the Home Office allows the right to work and other civil rights previously withheld.

Tito: Josip Broz Tito (1892–1980) was chief architect of the 'second' Yugoslavia that lasted from 1943 until 1991. Leader of the Partisan resistance during the Second World War, he went on to lead the Communist state of Yugoslavia until his death from post-surgery complications on 4 May 1980 in Ljubljana, Slovenia.

UDBa: The Yugoslav Secret Police that was the approximate equivalent of the KGB.

SELECT BIBLIOGRAPHY

Glenny, Misha, *The Fall of Yugoslavia*, Penguin Books, London, 1996

Glenny, Misha, *The Balkans*, Granta, London, 1999

Ibrahami, Ramadan N., *Masakra në Prapasticë dhe Keqekollë*, Blendi, Prishtinë, 1996

Judah, Tim, *The Serbs, History, Myth and the Destruction of Yugoslavia*, Nota Bene, Yale, 2000

Judah, Tim, *Kosovo, War and Revenge*, Nota Bene, Yale, 2002

Malcolm, Noel, *Kosovo, A Short History*, Macmillan, London, 1998

Murphy, Dervla, *Through the Embers of Chaos*, John Murray (Publishers) Ltd, London, 2002

Popovich, Stefan L., *Potovanja po Novoj Serbije*, Belgrade, 1950

Service, Robert, *Lenin*, Macmillan, London, 2000

Sherifi, Artan, *New Orientalism*, Unpublished Essay for Glasgow School of Art, 2004

West, Rebecca, *Black Lamb and Grey Falcon*, Macmillan, London, 1942

Aberdeenshire Library and Information Service
www.aberdeenshire.gov.uk/libraries
Renewals Hotline 01224 661511

03.   09.

- 6 NOV 2012

ABERDEENSHIRE
LIBRARIES
WITHDRAWN
FROM LIBRARY

27 MAR 2013

2 5 APR 2014

ABERDEENSHIRE
LIBRARIES
WITHDRAWN
FROM LIBRARY

SHERIFI, Remzije

Shadow behind
the sun

A L I S

2576498

Also by Robert Davidson

Poetry
The Bird & The Monkey
Total Immersion
After The Watergaw (Editor)
Columba (Poetry Scotland)
Butterfly on a Chestnut Leaf

Song Cycle
Centring on a Woman's Voice

Libretto
Dunbeath Water – an oratorio

Non-fiction
Uamhas! (SMC Yearbook 1994)
Winning Through (with Brian Irvine)
City of the Highlands
City of the Lowlands

Magazines
Northwords (Reviews Editor: 1998–2001)
Northwords (Managing Editor: 2001–2004)
Sandstone Review (Editor: 2004–2006)